FORGIVING
GOD

FORGIVING GOD

Embracing a Risky Adventure
With the Divine

Brian C. Macallan

PROCESS CENTURY PRESS
ANOKA, MINNESOTA 2023

Forgiving God: Embracing a Risky Adventure with the Divine

© 2023 Process Century Press

All rights reserved. Except for brief quotations in critical publications and reviews, no part of this book may be reproduced in any manner without prior permission from the publisher.

Process Century Press
RiverHouse LLC
802 River Lane
Anoka, MN 55303

Process Century Press books are published in association with the International Process Network.

Cover Design: Susanna Mennicke
Cover Photo: Furkan Güneş

Scripture quotations taken from The Holy Bible, New International Version® NIV®
Copyright © 1973, 1978, 1984, 2011 by Biblica, Inc.
Used with permission. All rights reserved worldwide.

VOLUME VI:
FAITH IN PROCESS
JEANYNE B. SLETTOM, GENERAL EDITOR

ISBN 978-1-940447-62-9
Printed in the United States of America

SERIES PREFACE: FAITH IN PROCESS

Alfred North Whitehead's process philosophy develops and explores the concept that all existence is necessarily relational. Nothing is isolated; all things are interconnected. Such theories are now commonplace in many of the sciences, but they are also deeply resonant with religious and theological thought. Perhaps the most profound religious expression of process thinking is the necessarily interrelational nature of all things, not only to one another, but also and centrally to God. Internally and externally, we exist in and through relationships. Many forms of process theologies have been developed in the decades since relational thinking deepened our understanding of reality.

Process Century Press has published a number of works dealing with relational thought. But theoretical work has not been the only mode of working with the relational structure of all existence—to the contrary, many practical implications have also affected personal and communal forms of religion. In this Faith in Process series, the Press looks to contemporary resources that enhance religious life, both personally and communally. It may well be that there is no greater need for such works than our present time. Given the flux in the contemporary world—the merging of politics and faith, renewed questions about who "qualfiies" to lead religious activities, tensions between freedom and responsibility, the scope of freedom for women and their own bodies, issues of migration, continuing racism—there are issues enough! Relational forms of thinking are needed now more than ever. And because we are indeed relational, interwoven with one another at our deepest levels, it may even be possible that works exploring and promoting our relationships to one another and to God may be part and parcel of our healing.

~Marjorie Hewitt Suchocki

OTHER BOOKS IN THIS SERIES

Praying with Process Theology, Bruce G. Epperly
The Call of the Spirit, John B. Cobb Jr., Bruce G. Epperly, Paul S. Nancarrow
Mystery without Magic, Russell Pregeant
Jesus Learns to Glow (picture book), Timothy Murphy and C.J. Ward
21 Psalms for the 21st Century, Marjorie Suchocki and Blair Gilmer Meek
Forgiving God, Brian C. Macallan

Contents

Preface, i

One: *Introduction: A Changing World*

Two: *Context and Cancer*

    When Cancer Came Knocking
    Chemotherapy
    A South African Christian
    Conversion

Three: *Collapse*

    Questions
    The Matrix (Clarity)

Four: *Why God Became a Problem*

    Authenticity and Anxiety
    Cancer and Evolution
    Camus, Revolt, and the Death of God
    Evolution and Theodicy
    Sin and Christology

Five: *Getting off the Omnibus: Progressing to Process Theology*

    First Explorations
    Getting off the Omnibus

Six: *Rethinking Reality*

    Theology Is Natural
    Reality as Event

             Reality as Relational and Interconnected
             Reality as Change and Process
             Summary

Seven: *Pathways to Process*

             Whitehead and Metaphysics
             Hartshorne and the Future
             Keller and Omnipotence
             Dombrowski and Experience
             Griffin and Panentheism
             Clayton and Emergence
             Summary

Eight: *Can the Real God Please Stand Up?*

             Where Is God?
             Does God Change?
             What Does God Know?
             What Can God Do?
             What Is God Like?
             Summary

Nine: *What Should We Be Doing? Joining the Adventure*

             Does God Have a Dream for the World?
             Global Crisis and Disorder
             The Impending Doom of Planet Earth
             Staying Engaged
             Communities and Zones of Resistance
             Small Turnings
             Political Promise
             Embodied Ethics
             Sustainability and Health
             Ethical Explorations (SHE)

Ten: *Embracing the Risk*

Notes

To Milla and Holly,
remain curious and open to the Divine.

Preface

THIS BOOK is about me, but also in some ways about you. It is about me in the sense that it attempts to chart the journey I have taken in my encounter with the divine and with the world. It is about you in the sense that I hope my journey offers you some worthwhile ideas to consider for your own journey in today's complex world. We are still dealing with the consequnces of a global pandemic that resulted in the deaths of hundreds of thousands of people. Australia, at the beginning of 2020, experienced its worst fire season on record as a result of human-driven climate change. The United States, in the wake of George Floyd's murder, continues to grapple with racial injustice and out-of-control gun violence. These are indeed unprecedented and challenging times.

This book is not only for people of faith, but for all of us who are committed to bringing about greater justice and sustainability on this planet. However, for myself, it is my faith and my encounter with God and the message of Jesus that have shaped my being, and therefore remain central to how I think about the world and my place in it. You might find certain things more helpful depending on where you are and what you are looking for. For those for whom God and the Christian faith are no longer relevant, I still hope that some of the proposals toward the end of the book regarding personal, communal, and political change will provide food for thought. And I will introduce you to a different way of thinking about questions of God and faith that I hope might entice you to reopen those questions, or at least stay with them a little longer.

There are different ways of thinking about the God-World relationship that can enable us to open ourselves up to both mystery and change, and I hope you will consider them in that spirit. For those who are already comfortable with some of my explorations around the nature of reality and God, I hope to give some very practical suggestions on how to participate in the adventure with the divine in creating a more just, merciful, and flourishing world. As the prophet Micah said, "to do justice, and to love kindness, and to walk humbly with your God" (Micah 6:8) should be central to our concerns as people of faith.

More than anything, I have tried to stay clear of philosophical, theological, and political jargon, and to the extent that I have succeeded time will tell! So much of my work to date has been academic in nature, and although important, that is not what I am hoping to achieve with this book. Hence, the majority of this book is written in the first person, with attempts to be as colloquial and accessible as possible. For those who want more substantive justifications, more technical language, or more avenues to pursue, I have provided further resources in the endnotes. The notes are more academic in this sense and provide material of a different nature than the body of the text. You could easily read the whole book through without reading the notes, and you would not be worse off for understanding the key thrust of the arguments. I do hope that you find this book helpful, and I thank you for taking the time to stop and listen to my journey in forgiving God and embracing a risky adventure with the divine.

Chapter One

Introduction: A Changing World

THE WORLD IS CHANGING. The world has always been changing. So has the universe, for that matter. In fact, since the universe began around 13.8 billion years ago we have moved from quantum fluctuations, to molecules, to single-celled organisms, to multicellular organisms, to complex forms of life, through animal life to human beings. Change and movement have been fundamental to the evolution of the universe and to life on this planet.

Our climate has changed, too, and has done so throughout the Earth's history.[1] Sadly, in more recent times, human beings have been directly responsible for this change, the result of which will be enormous suffering for human beings and other life-forms on the planet. Human evolution has not equipped us to think much beyond our next meal, hence the challenge to think a few years ahead, let alone a few centuries ahead, is enormously difficult.[2] Change is fundamental but, of course, not all change is good. It is easy to claim that these times are the *most* at risk and the *most* unsettled and the *most* tumultuous. We could point to the election of Trump, brutal dictatorships, Brexit, protests in Europe, climate change, and, more recently, COVID-19. And in some sense, the claim that today's crises are more dangerous than any previous era might be true. The existential threats of climate change and nuclear disaster are problems that could literally destroy us in a way that challenges of the past could not.[3] The pervasive nature of our current global issues, and the potential for our complete destruction, create challenges particularly unique to our era.

At the same time, though, there is much good in the world, and we have made significant progress on numerous fronts compared to previous generations. This is often hard for us to realize when we open our laptops and turn on our televisions.[4] But Yuval Noah Harari, citing research, evidence, and statistics, reinforces this more positive view. His general conclusion is worth noting,

> at the dawn of the third millennium, humanity wakes up to an amazing realization. Most people rarely think about it, but in the last few decades we have managed to rein in famine, plague and war. Of course, these problems have not been completely solved, but they have been transformed from incomprehensible and uncontrollable forces of nature into manageable challenges.[5]

It's easy to constantly criticize and be overly negative about our world situation, and such negativity can often lead to despair and hopelessness. Harari reminds us that celebrating the victories of the past, along with current progress, can create an important impetus to generate hope in the present and towards our future.

The universe changes, and the world changes. But so do we, as individuals. Our bodies are constantly changing and moving. The very cells that make up our body are constantly dying and regenerating every second. The "stuff" that made up our body a few years back has long since disappeared: We really are, literally, a new creation. Much of our body is different from the person we were even last year. In many ways it is our memory and neural networks, along with specific parameters given by our DNA, that continue to give shape, form, and consistency to who we are as individuals. But still, we change. For some of us this change can be more substantial than others. Whether it is changing friendship circles or moving countries, these experiences and new contexts influence and change our thinking, and hence our engagement with the world. I'm not suggesting that all change is good, nor that we should seek change for the sake of change. The point is that things are continually shifting around us and, as will become apparent later, this change, coupled with a divine invitation, is towards towards a generous and more open view of the world and our place in it. But in order to describe to you this possibility, I first need to take you on the journey I've been on.

I mentioned earlier the reality of change, and how it shifts and transforms even our identity. This has certainly been the case in my own life. Both the people and the ideas to which I have been exposed have shifted and changed the way I think about God, politics, and all things in between. Hence, the first part of this book will be an attempt to contextualize myself regarding my own history and faith odyssey. It will illustrate my journey from a fundamentalist Christian to someone who now embraces a process theological interpretation of Christian faith and practice. The first few chapters will discuss this theological shift and how some of the changes in my thinking were brought about by my cancer diagnosis and illness. This generated a new vision of God and my place in the world. Although different in some aspects from the Christian faith I inherited, I still believe it is consistent with the message of Jesus and God's dream for the world.[6]

It is this rethinking of the God-world relationship that I will attempt to articulate in the middle section of the book. I will argue that the vision of a God who is dynamically engaged with creation, who influences us and is in turn influenced by us, is core to a more hopeful outlook for our world. This vision will further challenge traditional assumptions of power and knowledge, which will reshape the way we think about our responsibility in and to the world and lead to some of my small suggestions at the conclusion of the book as to how we might live differently, with a more faithful practice.

Ultimately, it is a vision that asks us to join with God in the risky adventure of creating and participating in a new world of justice, hope, and forgiveness for all creation. You might not agree with the different ways I think about God (which challenge many core Christian theological positions), or necessarily agree with some of my proposals for how God engages with the world. I do hope, though, that you will at least "stray further afield" in being open to some of these ideas and practices. You may even consider participating with me in a risky adventure with the divine. So, in order to get the journey going, I need to begin with the event that (outside of my marriage and the birth of my two children) has shaped my life the most radically. It shifted everything in my life from the way I think about God to the eggs I buy at the grocery store. This was the arrival of cancer in 2013.

Chapter Two

Cancer and Context

I REMEMBER the day I was walking to my appointment to have a colonoscopy. I vividly remember the music I was listening to (Vega4). I even remember what I was thinking. We all have strange thoughts from time to time, but I clearly remember this one: "I hope they find something. I'm feeling super burnt out and it would be great to have a break from work."

When cancer came knocking

I honestly didn't expect them to find anything. I had gone for a checkup and had a range of blood tests done as a precaution the week before. Everything was good, and I had nothing to worry about. For reasons that have now become burdened with hindsight and conjecture, I asked the doctor if I could have a colonoscopy. It's highly unusual for a 35-year-old to request such a procedure. I mentioned that my dad had died from colon cancer (which he hadn't), realizing my chances of getting a referral were close to zero unless I had a real concern or family history (hence the lie about my dad). So that morning, when I was undergoing the colonoscopy (not the nicest procedure but compensated for by the cool feeling of the anesthetic), I was reasonably relaxed. When I woke up, the doctor asked me who had accompanied me. It was at this point that I began to realize something was amiss. I had been hoping to walk home, thinking the procedure no big deal. I lied again, saying my mom was coming to pick me up. He said that it was important someone was with me when we had our discussion around what he had found. I quickly phoned my mom who arrived around ten minutes later. It was a strange and surreal moment.

"You have a tumor" were the first words that came out of his mouth. He proceeded to tell me it was large, that it was almost blocking my colon, and that it had been difficult to finish the procedure. He then mentioned that I had to see my doctor again to wait for the results from a biopsy. Regardless of the results, I would have to have an operation to remove it. The initial results from the biopsy indicated that the tumor was in its early stages and likely *pre*cancerous. This was a relief, to say the least.

When I finally met the colorectal surgeon, and had another colonoscopy, he seemed to disregard the first test results. He said that from what he had seen it would be lucky if the tumor were at stage 1, but it was likely much worse. The next few weeks before the operation, I was reasonably upbeat about what lay ahead and found comfort in prayer and conversations. For whatever reason, I embarked on reading a biography of Tolstoy and a biography of Jung, and I spent time reading Hans Küng's book, *Does God Exist?*[1] Why these choices? I'm not sure. In reading Tolstoy I was reminded how death for people 100 years ago was so much more common and ever present. Back then people like Tolstoy would lose many of their children, and often at a young age. My eldest daughter Milla had contracted Legionnaires disease from her water birth and had almost died in her first month of life. My second daughter Holly had a staph infection following a burn in her second year. Both would have been dead in Tolstoy's time. I felt grateful. I read huge sections of Küng's book in a local graveyard prior to the operation. I agree, it's a little strange, but I always felt that being in a graveyard has helped me focus on the gift of being alive. I eventually booked in four weeks' sick leave from my role as lecturer in theology and prepared for what lay ahead.

Chemotherapy

Nothing really prepared me for the aftermath of the operation to remove two-thirds of my colon and the tumor within it. I had previously held ideas of a very luxurious recovery period and had therefore taken several books to the hospital in order to "work through them" when I woke up, and in recovery when I got home. After over a week in hospital, I left exhausted from a lack of sleep and too much morphine. Following the operation, I was unable to keep food down, and my weight dropped quickly. I now was 20kg lighter than my pre-operation weight. I began to slide into a sense of hopelessness and depression. I received a letter in the post requesting me to see the oncologist. It was all becoming very real. I read the letter, weeping from tiredness and fear. Since my diagnosis, I had frantically been trying to understand the different stages of colon cancer and its survival outcomes. At this point I knew I didn't have stage 4 colon cancer, as the CT scan prior to operation had shown no spread of the cancer to other organs.

My first meeting with the oncologist was strange, with me not really knowing what to expect. The results were a mixture of good and bad news. It was good in the sense that the cancer had not spread to my lymph nodes, but bad in that it had penetrated my colon wall. Hence I was classified with high-risk stage 2 colon cancer. The survival rate for this was around 70% after five years.

The oncologist recommended that I start chemotherapy that day and continue once a week for the next six months. By doing so I would increase my chances of survival by 25% to around 78%. Numbers, just numbers. I asked him rather naively what stage the cancer would be if it returned. When he mentioned stage 4 (the survival statistics of which I was well aware), it suddenly dawned on me that stage 2 wouldn't be happening again, and neither would a progression to stage 3. The consequences of a return were serious. That day I sat down in a room with around ten other cancer patients and began my first infusion of chemotherapy.

If I hadn't been diagnosed with colon cancer, it is unlikely I would have ever attempted to write this book. The event was what James Fowler calls an intrusive marker event. These are events that

> happen to us that affect our lives pervasively. They alter the patterns of our lives fundamentally. A marker event is one after which in some significant sense one's life is never the same again.[2]

The journey since getting cancer has seen my life unravel in multiple ways and in diverse areas. It has influenced everything from what I choose to eat, my beliefs about God, and how I spend my time and money. Everything has changed. This book charts the effect of cancer's advent into my life. It reflects on how my traditional understandings of Christian faith, and of who God is, could not bear the weight of the arrival of cancer. As the title of the book *Forgiving God* suggests, it also demonstrates how I have come to see God differently. The book describes my journey toward a different understanding of reality, which leads to a different understanding of God. It further shows how this new perspective on the divine is one that impacts not only myself, but how I understand my engagement with all of creation. It charts a way of living that, as the subtitle suggests, is *a risky adventure with the divine*. To understand these shifts, I need to describe the context in which my previous perspectives were shaped: I was formed as a white, straight, male, South African, charismatic Christian.

A South African Christian

I grew up under apartheid in South Africa. I was twelve years old when Nelson Mandela was released from prison and sixteen when the African National Congress (ANC) became the first democratically elected government in South Africa.[3] I was quite young and immature when these events were taking place. In fact, the most important thing about the relaxing of race requirements for my junior school was that our soccer team, with the influx of other races, became almost unbeatable overnight! Other schools that chose not to allow nonwhite students to attend suffered badly on the soccer field.[4] For me, the separation of races was broken down more easily through sport. Sport, as a unifying factor, was to play an important role in the future of South Africa, and it still does.[5]

Nelson Mandela's release from prison, along with the first multiracial elections, was both frightening and euphoric for South Africans. What would happen? Who would people vote for? The newly unbanned African National Congress? Or perhaps the old National Party government that had been in power since 1948? There were, of course, many options, but in my mind only one—the African Christian Democratic Party.

As a young fundamentalist Christian, it was as simple as forming a Christian worldview from the Bible and applying it to all of society in order to generate change. This assumption holds that the Bible is very clear about how it believes society should be structured and how that structure needs to be implemented. In hindsight, it was an attempt to take a static understanding of reality and apply it to a dynamic situation. But at the time, I had only just recently become a Christian, and I took all this stuff very seriously.

Conversion

I actually became a Christian by chance (or at least that's my story). I slept over at a friend's house one night and found myself at a Congregational Church and Sunday school the following morning. I enjoyed it and continued to attend. Eventually, one morning in the church hall, the Sunday school teacher asked if I wanted to give my life to Jesus.[6] This moment had been nicely primed by playing a phonograph record backwards. We were told it had secret satanic messages. I duly raised my hand and said a prayer to accept Jesus into my heart. The next question was whether I wanted to be baptized in the Holy Spirit and pray in tongues. For whatever reason that sounded cool and I went for that option, too. I was eleven years old at the time. The next few years saw me involved in everything church related. I attended church three times on Sunday and numerous Bible studies during the week.

An early intrusive marker event arrived on my doorstep when I was 15 years old, which would be my first encounter with cancer. My girlfriend at the time had a brother who was dying of cancer (he had leukemia and was 18 years old). I had been to my pastor, who had given me numerous verses to pray for his healing, and I had given them to my girlfriend as well. I remember the day he died, when she was called from the class. I felt confused about why God hadn't healed her brother. This was mixed with feelings of guilt regarding all the verses I had given her to pray for her brother's healing.

It didn't happen quickly, but the disillusionment eroded my faith, resulting in a drift away from church. I embraced a world of risky teenage experimentation involving drugs, sex, and alcohol. This didn't serve me particularly well, and I ended up entering my final year of high school with underwhelming grades. At a party one night in my final year of high school, I met a girl (my future wife). The night of our first kiss and conversation, I was high on drugs and she was one of several girls I kissed! She turned out to be a "missionary dater" who invited me to a Christian camp, where I made a recommitment in my faith and again found myself in a charismatic church.

My journey over the next ten years involved church again becoming my life. At the same time, at age nineteen, I began theological studies. As my education broadened, I eventually left behind many of my more extreme theological views (like the Catholic church being the whore of Babylon). My theological journey led me to the University of South Africa and then, finally, to Stellenbosch University. It is there that I eventually completed my doctorate in theology. In 2009, at 29 years of age, our family emigrated to Melbourne in Australia to lead a church. After four years pastoring, I began a role lecturing in theology.

In my first two years of lecturing, I journeyed far from my earlier fundamentalist and Pentecostal beginnings, and I could hardly be conceived as an evangelical conservative. My core convictions were largely intact, though, even if I had refused to open up areas in my theological thinking that I knew would be too risky in my college and church context. I hadn't yet allowed the reality of evolution, even if it was something I had endorsed, to fully challenge my thinking. I was two years into my new role as lecturer in theology when cancer came knocking.

Chapter 3

Collapse

My background is in practical theology. I was therefore well versed in helping students reflect on their pastoral concerns. *Start with your experience and your contextual reality, and then let that be the space from which you engage both the theological and cultural resources at your disposal.* In a very real sense, following the arrival of cancer, I was now my *own* pastoral concern.

Questions

Through the depression and anxiety I was experiencing post operation and diagnosis, I found myself coming to terms with the reality that if my cancer returned, my chances of survival were slim. I was asking questions about my existence that I had not previously asked; it was becoming an existential crisis. I thought I believed in an afterlife? I thought I had confidence in God to sustain me through trials and preserve my subjective immortality into the next life? Yet I was gripped with fear. I didn't want to leave my young daughters and wife behind. I liked living!

At this time, I met someone my age with three kids who had stage 4 colon cancer. I met with him four weeks before he died, and he still believed that God was going to heal him; hence he didn't feel the need to plan his goodbyes. I desperately admired and wanted his confidence. When he asked how I was finding things, I could only answer that I was terrified and did not have his confidence that God would intervene if I was in a situation similar to his.

I had been a Christian for over two decades, had been a church leader, and was now a lecturer in theology, yet my beliefs were as fragile as ever. I had intuitively known about the fragile basis for my faith, yet I had purposely chosen to ignore many of the biblical and theological difficulties I had encountered along the years. I had chosen to quarantine them, to put them in little bubbles, to keep them untouched and separated from the other parts of my thinking. I told myself that these were things I would come back to, but they needn't interfere too strongly with my present faith and practice. These questions concerned the implications of evolution for our understanding of sin and theodicy (the problem of evil in relation to God)[1] and the historical Jesus.

Just weeks before my diagnosis, I had been working through Karl Barth's *Church Dogmatics*. Post diagnosis and cancer, it seemed to lose all relevance to my life. As my existential crisis worsened, I tried re-reading N. T. Wright's *The Resurrection of the Son of God* and Moltmann's *Theology of Hope*. The reality, though, was that all the theological bubbles I had set up were beginning to burst. It's hard to know exactly when I felt I could no longer adhere to my previous understanding of God, and of how Jesus fitted into that picture. I think it happened after I read Albert Schweitzer's *Quest for the Historical Jesus*. I had read most of Wright's and Dominic Crossan's material on the historical Jesus. Both seemed to be rearranging the pieces to either end up with a conservative or a liberal Jesus. I finally read Dale Allison's *Historical Jesus and Theological*

Christ and realized that I needed to leave behind overhasty conclusions around Jesus from both the left and the right.

Whether or not these debates and authors are well known to you, the point is that certain scholars could no longer give me the security they had given me in the past. I was in uncharted territory. I needed new voices and ideas to help make sense of my experience.

If the truth were told, I had begun embracing a broader and more nuanced understanding of Christian theology decades before my diagnosis. Nevertheless, I had always felt that if I could just hold on to core Christian doctrines and how they are traditionally understood, I would be alright. I could still lead a church or teach theology. I had developed a range of mental gymnastics to help me with this, but I could no longer do this anymore. As certain aspects of my traditional beliefs collapsed, so did my faith. I felt a mixture of trepidation and relief.

The matrix (clarity)

Despite the enormous amount of anxiety and the existential crisis that followed my diagnosis, there emerged a strange clarity in how I saw myself in relation to the world around me. The best image I can use to describe this is from the first *Matrix* movie. There is a moment in the movie when the character Trinity is somehow able to freeze in midair before delivering a roundhouse kick. At this moment she is able to see all her assailants (and their bullets) with enormous clarity. Another image I used to describe my own clarity was of having previously been in a fog and not being able to see clearly the objects that surrounded me. You have a vague awareness of them at points, but then they vanish. You can also never see them all at the same time. Combining the two images above, it was as if a fog had lifted in my life, and I was now able to see everything around me clearly and in slow motion. This had nothing to do with literally seeing the world differently. It was more like being able to see clearly the things that were truly important. It was also clear that there were things getting in the way of me acknowledging what was important, and having the courage to change my life in light of this.

The most important clarifying moment for me was realizing how important my wife and children were to me. I had a deepening sense that relationships are crucial to a meaningful life, and that success, money, and reputation often get in the way of prioritizing relationships.[2] Does this feel like I am stating something obvious, something you already know and do? If so, look at your life and ask yourself what you spend your time and your money on. I realize that we are all in different financial and social situations, but it is still a useful exercise. Are we really prioritizing what is important?

One of my major clarifying moments was realizing that I spend too much time trying to keep other people happy and being anxious not to offend them.[3] This is linked directly to not being willing to confront the very real questions I have regarding God and faith. With the awareness that death might come at any point, I no longer felt a desire to please others as I previously had.[4] This enabled me to confront questions I had been asking and to bring them out into the open. More soberly, I realized that regardless of cancer, one day I will die, and that within two generations no one will really remember me. Why am I so concerned with people having a good opinion of me?

My driving desire became to live the one life I had and to live it well. I began to work less. As a family, we downsized our house in order to have more time and money for the things that really mattered.

Along with this shift to a more integrated and authentic way of living in faith and life, I was also rethinking my diet and health, which I will elaborate on more fully in chapter six. Suffice it to say, I began to read journal articles on cancer recurrence and how to prevent it.⁵ This coincided with an important insight that I came across from John O'Donohue. O'Donohue reminds us (often!) that our body is the only home we have in the universe.⁶ Combining a deep appreciation for my body, along with a desire to prevent a recurrence of cancer, I radically changed what I ate. I cut out most sugars that aren't natural, avoided red meat, and tried to eat more organically. Eventually, I became a vegetarian. I also tried to integrate some of these decisions into broader commitments concerning my faith and my understanding of God.

The year following my diagnosis resulted in an intensive and frantic reading around themes related to the historical Jesus, cancer, evolution, and theodicy. It is over this time that God became a problem for me, which eventually led me to endorse a more radical understanding of God.

Chapter 4

Why God Became a Problem

Many Christians, and people in general, tend to disregard information that doesn't gel with their current views or their understanding of things they deem most important. There are numerous psychological explanations for this, such as confirmation bias and cognitive dissonance.[1]

Authenticity and anxiety

Cognitive dissonance is when individuals who hold specific beliefs find themselves challenged by another belief that contradicts the one they currently hold. In this scenario, the individual experiences mental discomfort (dissonance) and must relieve the tension by either finding a way to dismiss the new view or moving toward integrating and embracing it. Many people find it easier to dismiss the new evidence in favor of their currently held and cherished beliefs. This could be for many reasons, such as not wanting to cause tension in relationships with friends and family members who might be threatened by the challenge to their beliefs. It could be for financial and work reasons, such as pastors not wanting to lose their job in a church.

Confirmation bias is perhaps more troubling, in the sense that as human beings we tend to seek out information that confirms our views. Here we tend not to read newspapers that might support a different political persuasion, or not to read theological books that are not aligned with our theology. This makes it difficult even to get into a situation where cognitive dissonance could happen. I contend that this is one of the main reasons why individuals should study in a formal setting, and not just follow their own reading plan. It's more likely that in a college or university scenario the lecturer would be abreast of current scholarship and also assign individuals with alternative views. Sadly, though, this is not often the case, and often it is not even possible due to the cost of university education and the time needed to pursue it.

I, like everyone else, am prone to confirmation bias, and I battle with cognitive dissonance. But my quest for a more authentic and honest way of living was fast-tracked with the arrival of cancer. So what was it specifically about cancer that would challenge me, not only with regard to living a more holistic and balanced life, but also challenge the core features of my theology?

Cancer and evolution[2]

The tumor inside me was the result of a mutation in the DNA of a cell in my colon that escaped my body's usual protective repair processes. Over time the cell began to multiply uncontrollably and with a destructive capacity. Most of our cells should naturally commit apoptosis, cell suicide. When this doesn't happen, the resulting cell growth becomes a problem. In my case, this was not only a problem of physical health and survival, but also a theological and philosophical problem.

It is paradoxical that the process of genetic mutation in a replicating cell can lead both to cancer and to the evolution of new life. Sadly, a virus like COVID-19 is a negative feature of a process that also led to our existence as the human species. The evolution of life from an original, single-celled organism to the complex forms we see today is the result of a genetic mutation in those cells that resulted in an advantage for that organism. As John Polkinghorne points out, cancer is the trade-off we must accept for a life that creates itself in new forms.[3] Taking both evolution and God seriously, one could speculate regarding a scenario wherein God hardwired this mechanism into creation to be its vehicle for progress. What would this say about God? These mutations can allow a selective advantage for certain species to prevail over others. If, as Polkinghorne suggests, God has allowed cell mutation as a mechanism for the world to create itself, with cancer and COVID-19 as potential byproducts, it seems that God has endorsed suffering and pain in order for life to evolve. Even, dare I say it, that God has *created* suffering and pain. As Jung reminds us, a flowery meadow is also a slaughterhouse wherein insects and animals compete for survival.[4] What is this world that God has created?

According to the Pew Research Center, evolution is affirmed by almost 98% of biologists and 95% of scientists.[5] Despite this, more than four in ten Americans continue to believe that God created humans in their present form 10,000 years ago, a view that has changed little over the past three decades. Half of Americans believe humans evolved, with the majority of these saying God guided the evolutionary process.

In Australia, the difference between Christians and the general population is stark. According to the Nielson poll on faith, only 12 percent of Australian Christians believe in evolution through natural selection, with 38% of Christians rejecting it. Eighty-nine percent of those who do not believe in God agree with Darwin's theory of natural selection.[6]

By the age of 19, after completing two years of Bible college at a fundamentalist institution, I was convinced of a 10,000-year-old world, a literal Adam and Eve, and original sin, as served up by my then-hero, American evangelical theologian Francis Schaeffer. Broadly, sin might be understood as disobedience against God, with original sin being defined as the view that human sin entered the world through the disobedience of Adam and Eve. Original sin is something that forever impacted the world, and it is something from which we cannot escape.

My first crisis was as a 20-year-old beginning my first-year studies in theology and reading Hans Küng's book *Credo*.[7] My thinking began to shift. Initially, I dismissed Küng as the Anti-Christ, but my views softened as I realized that other evangelicals believed in evolution[8]—they just saw God as part of this process. It was also at this time that I read John Stott's little book on *Understanding the Bible*,[9] wherein he writes of a first hominid couple, and then C. S. Lewis's accounts of theistic evolution.[10] Neither are dissimilar to N. T. Wright, mentioned earlier, who called for an original hominid couple. In truth, though, I never seriously worked out the implications of what evolution would actually mean for any of the traditional Christian doctrines I had inherited. I had previously found it more helpful to emphasize a perspective that focused on Jesus's role in overcoming not so much sin, but rather the reality of death. With some of my inhibitions dissipating, and my compartmentalized thinking being challenged through my encounter with cancer, I began to read as much as I could on evolution and its intersection with theology and ethics.

The science is compelling. Since the creation of the universe some 13.8 billion years ago, reality has transitioned from a quantum to an atomic realm, from chemical properties to single-celled, then complex multicellular life, moving to ever more sophisticated organisms, and eventually to consciousness. Evolution by natural selection has largely been responsible for the transition on the biological side of life. As Alistair McGrath tells us, the science is one thing, the metaphysical freighting one places on it, another.[11] It is not my desire to engage in whether theism or atheism is a better explanation of these data.[12]

Making moral judgments on events in the present is an enormous difficulty, let alone the past, especially when it comes to evolution. The destructive and creative capacities for life have early origins in exploding stars that provided the raw material for all of life as we now experience it. As chemical reactions formed in the underwater geysers of the planet some 4.3 billion years ago, cellular life began to emerge and multiply. We know precious little of this early life, the first glimpses of which are in the Burgess shale and the appearance of the first tiny creatures, possibly ancestors of the first vertebrate.[13] We then have a real explosion of life during the Cambrian era. From that point, we can begin to track large portions of the evolutionary process, first in the fossil record and later with the genome project, which tracks the DNA history and evolution of many living organisms. The history of evolution demonstrates that death entered the cellular world early on, in the transition from single-celled to multicellular organisms. The trade-off for this diversity was individual cell death. Problematically, some cells, due to mutations in their DNA, fail to die and instead replicate into new cells with increasing levels of DNA error. Hence the tumor that would arrive for me! It is this cell division process in the reproductive cells and in their mutations—at least the ones that don't kill you—that can provide a selective advantage in one's environment, leading to a higher probability of propagation of the species. This gives a richer meaning to Nietzsche's phrase, "What doesn't kill you makes you stronger."

Species lacking the advantage that a specific mutation may once have provided eventually cannot compete and are either killed off or die out. What is clear is that this death is not by any stretch of the imagination the punishment for sin, as the Apostle Paul imagined it, nor, for that matter, is it an obstacle Jesus needed to conquer as something alien to the process of life. If anything, it is the mechanism by which creation moved itself forward into more complex forms of life. If we have a God who predetermines the process of evolution, or at least foreknows that it will take place, we are faced with a God who is ultimately and primarily responsible for death, suffering, and some of the difficulties that result in moral sin.[14]

Camus, revolt, and the death of God

My journey into questions of theodicy in connection to cancer and evolution led me to deeply concerning questions regarding God's involvement in the world. The profound challenge of a God who would knowingly create a universe with such violence at the core of the creative process was, and is, problematic for me. Of course, traditional forms of Christianity often presuppose a creation that fell into disorder and sin due to the Fall (the original disobedience of Adam and Eve). This form of Christianity allows God off the hook, so to speak. This has never been a valid option for me.

If God is an all-knowing and all-powerful being, it appears difficult, to me, that God should (1) begin a process knowing what the outcome will be (with its attendant suffering); (2) have the power to change it; yet (3) allow it to happen anyway This problem has been classically formulated by the philosopher David Hume:

> Is he [God] willing to prevent evil, but not able? then is he impotent. Is he able, but not willing? then is he malevolent. Is he both able and willing? Whence then is evil?[15]

Within a year of my diagnosis and the collapse of my traditional understanding of Christian faith, I was still wrestling deeply with my understanding of God. What is this world that God has created?

I read Camus' *Revolt*, during a weekend away, after I finished my chemotherapy. I had originally bought the book hoping it was a novel like the other Camus books I had read. It was not that! At the time, it was his chapter on the metaphysical revolt against God that was most moving. Camus beautifully discusses the story in Dostoevsky's *Brothers Karamazov*, where Alyosha's brother challenges him whether it is legitimate and justified to create a world, even if you have to sacrifice one baby to make that happen.[16] Alyosha says no. Camus, reflecting on this dialogue in Dostoyevsky, notes that this does not result in disbelief or rejection of God necessarily. It does, however, result in a rejection of the world, with all its attendant suffering, that God has created.[17]

Christian theology, at least in its Augustinian tradition, has argued that sin and suffering entered the world through the disobedience of Adam and Eve—the classic doctrine of original sin. This seems to be the argument of Paul in Romans 5 that leads him directly to the mission of Jesus. Adam and Eve sinned, therefore all have sinned. And then, through one man, Jesus, we are redeemed (the doctrine of atonement, variously understood).[18]

Not all Christians believe this, but certainly many do. It has led N. T. Wright to argue for some kind of original primal hominid couple chosen by God as central to Christian faith.[19] I have come, however, to agree with Hebrew Bible scholar Peter Enns that we need to leave behind Paul's understanding of the cause of sin and death.[20] This includes rejecting strange accounts of the first hominids as human representatives, as Wright proposes. According to Enns, and I agree, this would have been a very foreign creature to Paul.[21] Regardless of whether some primal couple existed, which to me seems rather strange, Wright's solution raises far more complex problems than a literal Adam and Eve does. Allowing something to evolve that clearly has dramatic faults inherent in its survival strategy, in a world that God created to evolve in this manner, is like blaming a computer for a software issue when the problem is clearly a hardware one. And here is the difficulty for me: in this view, humans—some representative primal evolved human pair—cannot be responsible for sin and suffering, as this would always have been present. We are the imperfect products of an evolutionary process that has left us with certain dispositions and desires, and some of these dispositions and desires have led to many of the moral sins we now experience. Furthermore, it does not appear that there was any specific point in time where we were sufficiently liable to be responsible for an ultimate sin towards God. So, is it God who is perhaps responsible for sin and suffering? Is it God who is in need of forgiveness? These are incredibly troubling questions for many of us within the Christian tradition.

Ultimately, I found myself in the strange position of still believing in some form of ultimate reality, but not the traditional God of my Christian faith. This all-powerful and all-knowing God seemed a tyrant, and more irresponsible than any half-decent parent would be. I revolted because I was revolted. It was sickening.

Jewish philosopher Hans Jonas has penetratingly articulated this question in his essay *God after Auschwitz*. Jonas had to leave Nazi Germany early in Hitler's reign, yet later returned as a soldier fighting for the British army. He searched for his mother on his return, but she had been gassed in Auschwitz. He vowed never to live in Germany again. Jonas asked the probing question regarding the God I was revolting against: "What is the matter with God that he would allow Auschwitz to happen?" For him, "Only a completely unintelligible God can be said to be absolutely good and absolutely powerful, yet tolerate the world as it is."[22]

Evolution and theodicy

The reality of sin and suffering is complicated by Christian ideas of original sin—a moral corruption introduced by the disobedience of

Adam and Eve and subsequently inherited by every human being. N. T. Wright believes that, although Adam and Eve are not literal figures, it remains important to affirm some primordial couple whereby some form of original sin is introduced into humankind. For Dale Migliore, however, starting with Adam and Eve won't do. He doesn't question the universality of sin (the "whole of humanity finds itself in a condition or state of captivity to sin"[23]), but the challenge to him, then, is when and where did this captivity take place?

I believe we are born prone to sin, but we are not ultimately responsible for the existence of sin, suffering, and death in the world. This is not to say that as growing, moral, and ethical beings, having evolved consciousness, we cannot be held accountable for our actions. However, in an ultimate sense God, as the creator of life, remains responsible for the universe. Evolution has as its drivers both death and the competition for those resources necessary for survival. Both lead ultimately to suffering. The more complex creatures become, and the more conscious, the more painful the suffering and our awareness of it becomes. Should we revolt against this God, as Camus suggests? Should we reject this world, as Aloysha does?

I listened to an interview with Elie Wiesel, just after I finished chemotherapy, in which he was asked about something he wrote in his book *Night*. In it he said that when he saw the young children going up in flames in a concentration camp, his faith went up in flames. When asked what he did next, he answered "I continued to pray. It's not that I don't believe in God, I am just angry with him."[24]

In a similar manner, my theological and existential wonderings had led me—if God is indeed ultimately responsible for sin—to consider the question of whether God is malicious, negligent, or limited. And if so, what does this mean for the mission of Jesus as a response to sin? Like Wiesel, I wanted to pray, but I also wanted to be honest.

Sin and Christology

I was hesitant to admit the implications of these musings for my Christology, especially as I had been taught to understand it. First, I would have to select, from any of the several versions available, which version of the historical Jesus to engage. Is it the historical Jesus of Dominic Crossan, the wandering cynic?[25] Is it the Jewish Jesus of Wright, who in some dark and mysterious way believes himself to be Israel's King returning?[26] Is Jesus the apocalyptic prophet of Dale Allison (following Albert Schweitzer)?[27] Or would I be simply burning myself on the critical fires, as Bultmann suggests, by even asking these questions?[28] Perhaps the above names will be unfamiliar, but simply naming them captures the point: Questions about the historical Jesus are contested amongst scholars.

Personally, I am not convinced there is any one picture of Jesus that emerges from the New Testament documents, but I sympathize most with Allison's view. Given my thesis—that human beings cannot be held responsible for sin in the way that the doctrine of original sin suggests, I had to exclude the idea of Jesus having to die for our sins, or needing to conquer death because we or some primal human couple sinned. I needed to rethink the role of sin and death, because death has been present from the origins of life.

This perhaps flies in the face of much New Testament teaching, but it would seem to be a natural implication. Perhaps Pierre Teilhard de Chardin's view of a Christ who emerges as the Omega point of creation needs to be revisited, although, as critics have pointed out, his strong teleological view runs into problems with the randomness of the evolutionary process.[29] Perhaps God waited for the right moment to become present in Christ? Waiting until a certain point in history to nullify death which, until then, had been so necessary to God's unfolding creation? There are many questions to ask here, but, for me, they had to reflect the reality that death and sin are not due to any privation of an original good, or a primeval fall, but are the result of the mechanisms that have driven life in order for free creatures to evolve. There are no easy answers to very difficult questions.

With all these questions now present, I needed to reorient myself. Cancer had thrown open many of the questions that I had been neatly neglecting. The challenges that were being raised with regard to traditional orthodox teachings were problematizing my understanding of God and faith. I entered a spiritual winter and a resulting loss of hope. It is at this point when I began to think about process theology again. Perhaps I could find hope in my winter?

Chapter 5

Getting off the Omnibus: Progressing to Process Theology

PROCESS THEOLOGY is seen by many to be an eccentric area within theology. Many could go through their whole undergraduate studies in theology and not come across any form of process thinking. This is unfortunate, as process theology has tackled some of the most important questions around the nature of reality and God. In this chapter, I will discuss key aspects of process thought in terms of how it challenges some traditional thinking around how we understand God, and how that was important for my journey with cancer.

First explorations

Process philosophy, and the work of Alfred North Whitehead in particular, could be going through a renaissance period. (I will introduce Whitehead in more detail shortly.) Didier Debaise argues that this renewed interest in Whitehead is because the speculative and cosmological questions he was asking have become central to current concerns today.[1]

Process philosophy got a foothold in North America during Whitehead's years of teaching at Harvard University. Charles Hartshorne, at the University of Chicago, and John B. Cobb, Jr., at Claremont School of Theology, further contributed to the engagement with process philosophy in the American setting. More recently, there has also been a strong interest in process thinking in certain parts of Asia, particularly China.[2] Process thought is also finding fresh expression in Europe, which can be seen in the formation of various associations in the last few years.[3] This revival in process thought might arguably be equated with the revival of interest in Henri Bergson,[4] long considered one of the forerunners of process philosophy. This is matched by an increasing interest in the work of Whitehead amongst those working in French philosophy.[5]

Process theology today has many proponents, all with different levels of allegiance to historical process theism. The renewed interest in panentheism today argues for the importance and relevance of engaging with process theology. Panentheism is the view that God is neither identical with nor limited to the world, but that God is nevertheless in the world and the world is in God. If I were to hazard some broad introductory statements on process thought, it would be that it offers a panentheistic approach to understanding the God-world relationship. This approach helps deal with some of the more difficult questions regarding the nature of God. It is a concept that takes seriously the nature of reality and builds speculatively upon that, calling forth a human response to participate with God in creating a better world for all.

My first encounter with process thought was through the evangelical theologian Stanley Grenz. I was on a beach in South Africa as a young 21-year-old reading his book *Renewing the Centre*. In the book he deals with the evangelical theologian Clark Pinnock, who had embraced some of the key insights of process theology. Pinnock concluded that human freedom implies that God's knowledge of the future is limited, because truly free human beings would be co-determinants, in the moment, of whatever the next moment becomes; that is, the "future" does not exist until it happens. Therefore it cannot be known ahead of time, even by God.

Clark Pinnock and Open Theism[6] (the evangelical version of process theology) made so much intuitive sense to my experience and my engagement with God that I let go of divine foreknowledge relatively easily. Only much later, roughly two years before my cancer diagnosis, did I read Cobb and Griffin's book *Process Theology: An Introductory Exposition*. There was much to be excited about in the book, but I confess to being totally bewildered by the weird world and vocabulary of Whitehead! Most distressingly, I remember feeling angry that their version of a process God could not *guarantee* a more just future for this life, let alone the next. Following cancer and my rethinking around God, I came to endorse wholeheartedly the concluding pages of that book. In their ending Cobb and Griffin argue that if the traditional portrait of God simply returning to fix everything at some point in the future is true, it means that "there is in fact no real danger." If all is "in the hands of a good and omnipotent God who will care for us, then the urgency disappears." They argue that there is no divine action apart from creaturely action. "The one who experiences the joy of this participation in the divine life hopes urgently for success, but accepts the risk that the only reward may be in the joy itself."[7]

It was two years after reading that book that I was diagnosed with cancer, and all the doubts and questions that had been brewing for some time opened up. It was only then that I began engaging more substantively with the questions that process theology had raised for me. In the previous chapter I discussed the deep questions that cancer raised in terms of theodicy, evolution, and sin. I now need to pick up the journey where I left off and illustrate how process theology gave me the language to navigate the territory I needed to traverse. Only then could I move forward in my faith.

Getting off the omnibus[8]

At some point I found myself asking, "Why God? Why do it this way?" Isn't God's absence the elephant in the room? New Testament scholar Dale Allison captures this beautifully: *God is like a child who does not know that the game of hide and seek is up!*[9] Perhaps process theology could help me make sense of this. Although diverse in scope and practice, process theology seeks to ameliorate some of the difficulties raised by questions like mine by rejecting God's omnipotence and foreknowledge of the future.[10]

Divine omnipotence is problematic for many reasons implicit in this narrative so far. If God is all-powerful, God is also all-responsible. The implications of this are unavoidable and generate even more questions: Is God responsible for cancer? Is God responsible for COVID-19? Is God responsible for the worst atrocities in history? Is God responsible for the Australian bushfires? Process theology says no, rejecting the view that God has all power by affirming that all things that exist have some form of power. Power is shared: "God never has a monopoly."[11] God's power can be described as something that "influences all that happens but determines nothing."[12]

Ultimately, God does not stand outside the flow of reality, but within it. In a panentheistic sense, God experiences all that every moment of reality experiences. God carries within God's self all the knowledge that has gone before and that now currently exists. However, as God has not yet experienced the future, each experience for God is new. Because we are free creatures, God does not know which option we will take, but God invites us to choose the best option for that moment toward the flourishing of creation.

Stephen Evans believes that process theology resolves *some* problems of evil in the world by suggesting either God's power or goodness, or both, are limited.[13] However, he cautions that this is a major modification of traditional theism. Evans misunderstands process theism in claiming that it posits God's goodness as limited. Griffin demonstrates that the existence of evil "does not contradict the belief that the supreme power of the universe is perfectly good, because this power is not the sole power."[14] Process theology defends omni-benevolence, rejecting the idea that the greatest conceivable being is lacking in goodness. This God is both wholly wise and good and cannot do evil.[15]

Like Evans, John Hick rejects process thought, particularly in his earlier works, because it is so apparently distinct from Christian faith and belief.[16] Whether this is true or not, what is more important for me is whether it accurately represents current understandings of science and religious experience, along with theological positions that might emerge from those discussions. If God knew that God would create a universe that would ultimately lead to so much suffering and pain—and in this case there is a certain subjectivity as to whether pain and suffering outweigh the joys and pleasures of living—then I find this hard to accept. Griffin has argued that traditional theism's assertion that God allows suffering is problematic when fused with the idea of divine foreknowledge.[17] If God knew that this world would have the degree of suffering it does, why did God not choose a better world? Yet it seems apparent that for free conscious life to have evolved, God would have to have allowed for the possibility of suffering. Griffin notes the enormity of this decision—that it is indeed a risky business.[18] God is neither the sole power nor all-powerful in the traditional sense, because God's power is persuasive and invitational, not coercive; therefore, we have the world that we do. It does seem to me, in light of the cosmological constants,[19] the rationality of the world, and religious experience, that some not-less-than-personal God had some form of conscious life in mind. Would this have been a reptilian consciousness if an asteroid hadn't destroyed the dinosaurs? If, as Stephen Jay Gould suggests,[20] you wound the universe all the way back to the beginning, would it unfold along different lines? It nevertheless seems very likely that some rational, conscious, free life would have evolved.[21] God, then, ultimately takes a risk in generating life. It is an act of faith, trust, and love on God's part to move creation forward.

If, however, God was able constantly to intervene in the world and tinker with things, then surely God would be morally bound to intervene at all times; particularly, in the case of needless suffering. If God did this, we would not be free, and God would be even more morally liable. Personally, I am grateful to be alive on this planet, grateful I found my cancer by chance, and grateful I did not, like two friends of mine, die young and leave their kids fatherless.

I found myself asking the terribly troubling and dark question: *Is it I who need to offer grace and forgiveness to this God?* Perhaps in generating all this suffering, God did not know what God was doing. Perhaps the God of classical theism has never really existed in the first place? Process theology articulates an understanding of divine reality that locates us within a God who suffers with us, a God who is literally affected by our engagement in the world, and who, despite our suffering, invites us into a future that is open, with all the risks and opportunities that it must, by definition, entail.

Before we get into the nuts and bolts of what process theology can offer us, we need to make a slight detour into physics and its description of reality. I have tried to keep this next chapter both short and accessible, but you may choose to skip it and go straigtht into the next. However, so much process thinking is based on a scientific description of reality that it helps to take a short excursion into science. The goal is to emerge with a picture of reality in which everything is an interconnected series of events in a continual process of change.

Chapter 6

Rethinking Reality

WHEN WE SPECULATE on God and on God's relationship with ourselves and the universe, we need to consider scientific perspectives not only on evolution but on the nature of the universe and reality itself. This brings us into the realm of metaphysics, which, simply put, is the attempt to describe the nature and structure of reality. Metaphysics has many facets, from trying to understand the nature of the relationship between body and mind to exploring the implications of quantum physics on our understanding of the universe.

Theology is natural

Throughout the ages religious believers have sought to position themselves against scientific views, not allowing scientific advances and discoveries to bring adjustments to their own perspective on the world. Take Galileo, for example, whose articulation of a heliocentric solar system was seen to be in conflict with the church's teaching,[1] or the long debate concerning evolution and its rejection by certain components of the church.

Tripp Fuller suggests that his faith is willing to go beyond science, but not below it. I think that is about right. Of course, what going "beyond" or "below" science means is open to debate, opinion, and the changing nature of scientific theory. But for me, going below science would be saying that the Earth is only 5000 years old and that God created humankind as a one-off event with Adam and Eve. Going beyond science would be to say that God might somehow have set up the initial conditions of the universe for life to evolve. It's not something we can empirically verify, but it's not going against any of the evidence, either. And going beyond science (making metaphysical statements about God and the world), is not something only religious people are prone to do! Richard Dawkins, by describing genes as "selfish," is going beyond science and making a speculative, metaphysical statement. As Alistair McGrath suggests, we are all prone to bringing our own metaphysical freight to the scientific evidence in our discussions.[2]

In this chapter, I suggest there are three aspects of reality that we need to take into account in trying to make sense of our faith and practice. These are key aspects that process theology has also sought to affirm in its deliberations. They are: reality as event, reality as process/change, and reality as relational. The second and third aspects have been particularly important for process theologians and will form the basis for comments I make regarding the God-World relationship.

These aspects are in line with Alfred North Whitehead, one of the most important process philosophers. Philosophy makes a distinction between empiricism and rationalism, as the former is limited to direct sensory observation of the world and the latter involves claims that can be logically posited, but cannot be objectively verified. Most philosophers are one or the other. Whitehead, unusally, was both. Moreover, he was a *radical* empiricist[3]; that is, relationality was crucial to his undertanding. We can describe a thing we see, hear, feel, etc., but the description is only partial unless we also describe how it is related to other things.

Whitehead began by asking how reality must be structured to allow for not only all manner of experience, but specifically for the quantum relationality of Einstein's new theory of relativity. If, in quantum mechanics, everything in the universe is interconnected, and if, theologically speaking, God is part of the universe, then perhaps we, too, are connected to God and all of creation.

Although it can feel counterintuitive, it is instructive to consider the nature of reality and then to ask what insight this offers on the nature of the divine. Surely, if God is involved in the universe and its unfolding, we should be reflecting on who God is and on God's motives for creating the universe?[4] Many Christian theologians reject attempts of this kind to say anything meaningful about the nature of God from the starting point of reality. They believe this is simply a form of "natural theology" and should be rejected out of hand. Natural theology often gets a bad rap for saying more than it can and less that it should.

Other Christians are terrified of looking at the natural world and the universe. They believe that the destructive aspects of nature and the more frightening aspects of evolution should be put into a box and kept shut. But I believe this is exactly what should be confronted in trying to understand who God is, along with what matters to God. Inside the box is a hidden treasure, the most beautiful show on Earth.[5] It is a tragic treasure. Process thought's valuable insight is that reality constrains not just us, but also God.

Process theologians focus on reality as relational and in process, i.e., as event. *Reality as event* is a remarkable idea regardless of any application to God; it is also both real and relevant for process thought.[6] We need to remember that often when we engage with the universe and the way reality is structured, it might feel counter-intuitive. The Earth seems flat, yet we know it to be round.[7] It feels like we are standing still, but the earth is spinning at 1300km/h and travelling through the universe at 23km a second! We also know that the sun doesn't revolve around the Earth, even when it feels like it does. Much of this overturns common assumptions about the way the world works and our common sense perception of reality.

For process theologians, the way the universe and reality are understood provides insight into the God-world relationship. The first aspect of reality we will affirm is that reality is event.

Reality as event

"A rock is an event."~Carlo Rovelli[8]

The astrophysicist Carlo Rovelli asks us to imagine a world where things are not made of substances, but rather are comprised by the relationship between quantum events. What would be so radical about considering reality as event? For one, an event is something that is happening, something that is not simply static. An event implies energy, a movement. An event that is dynamic is one that is given to change. Change and process. These are central concepts that process theology wrestles with and, as we shall soon see, have an impact on how we conceive God in relation to both power and knowledge.

Rovelli, when describing the fundamental aspects of nature, declares the universe is "nothing but change," and that events at the quantum level are central to a change that is ubiquitous. He argues that "things happen" and that

> The entire evolution of science would suggest that the best grammar for thinking about the world is that of change, not of permanence. Not of being, but of becoming. We can think of the world as made up of things. Of substances. Of entities.

Of something that is. Or we can think of it as made up of events. Of happenings. Of processes. Of something that occurs. Something that does not last, and that undergoes continual transformation, that is not permanent in time.[9]

Nuclear physicist John Jungermann helps us understand these "eventful changes" that Rovelli describes by looking at what is happening within an atom: the atom itself is a series of events. For Jungermann, the process philosophy of Whitehead is deeply consistent with the way reality is structured. Here is Jungermann's description of what is happening at the atomic level:

> the "empty" atom is filled with virtual pairs and also with photon and gluon force carriers that are continually being birthed and dying—a dynamic, creative process at the most elementary level of matter. So solid matter is not really solid at all, but empty; at the same time it is filled with dynamic radiation, or a "complex of events" in the language of process philosophy. Substance is really an effect of our macroscopic human senses; at the microscopic level the world is a series of events—a process.[10]

I remember reading this for the first time and battling to get my head around it! The point Jungermann is making, which is what Rovelli is also suggesting, is that reality is an interconnected series of events. If they are right, this interconnectivity will have implications for how we understand God and our relation to God. What is important to note at this point is that process philosophers are right in affirming that the idea of a static substance is not an adequate description of reality. And if God is part of this reality, then this would apply to God, too. We will talk more about this in the next chapter.

Didier Debaise is a French philosopher who has been part of the revival in Whitehead studies in Europe. In his key text *Nature as*

Event, he argues that all of Whitehead's philosophy is a "vast inquiry into the notion of event."[11] Whitehead used Cleopatra's needle (a concrete obelisk in London at Charing Cross) as an example to think about events and how they relate to change. We could equally use the Statue of Liberty or the Sphinx to think about the same concept. Debaise unpacks this eloquently:

> the continuity of the existence of the obelisk is an event that is not, in principle, so different from other occurrences within nature. The result, however, is important. If we agree with Whitehead, then all "things" of our experience—material objects, physical objects, whether technical or biological—are events that manifest similar principles of passage and temporal transition. Whitehead's position displays a willingness to place all objects, in so far as they persist, within the domain of events.[12]

If at a fundamental level events can be seen as primary, is there anything we can say about how, or if, these events are related to one another? For, often, when we think about an "event," we think of it as something that is separate from other things that are happening. However, we shouldn't think about events in this way, but rather begin to think about their interconnectedness. This leads to the second aspect of reality.

Reality as relational and interconnected

One of the key insights of modern science is that the universe is interconnected and interrelated. It is implied by both the general theory of relativity and quantum mechanics.[13] This is specifically something that astrophysicist Rovelli asserts, along with its potential implications; namely, that there are no isolated facts, and interrelatedness is one of the most fundamental aspects of nature itself.[14]

This insight, that we are all interconnected, might feel counterintuitive. We might look out the window right now and see a tree in the garden. Because we tend to think spatially, we quite "rightly" perceive that the tree is separate from us and think of it as a separate substance. Remembering that everything is actually an event, we must now think of the whole universe as an unfolding series of events and that everything is connected—we are connected, the tree is connected. Whitehead referred to this whole movement of the universe as the extensive continuum. We are moving though time relatively, and therefore experiencing time differently, but we are all in the process of duration, regardless.

One of the forerunners of process thinking was the French philosopher Henri Bergson. Bergson felt that one of the main problems in our thinking was that we tend to think of the world and the universe as substances in space. He encouraged us rather to think of all things being in the process of duration and movement. This becomes much easier when you think of the world as energy. Bergson gave many examples of what this might look like, but one that I've found particularly helpful is the image of trains on a track. In this image, Bergson asks us to imagine three train tracks running parallel to one other, with trains moving at high speed. If we were to stick out our hand to a friend in the train next to us we would still be moving, but we would also still be next to each other. We therefore ought to imagine the tree, ourselves, and the house next to us as being in movement on parallel train tracks. The train analogy helps us understand our joint movement but does not help us understand our connectedness. At an atomic, or fundamental level, we are interconnected. The event of the tree in some way affects the event that is me.

Reality as change and process

Process philosophers have argued over the years for the nature of process and change. We look around us, even at our bodies, and we see the constant shift and change that unfolds. As mentioned earlier, the Greek philosopher Heraclitus said that we never step into the same river twice. Evolution itself is a testament to the enormous shifts and development that life has progressed through, let alone the universe. The universe has, since the Big Bang, changed and developed from quanta, to atoms, to molecules, to single celled organisms, to complex life forms, to human beings with conscious minds. I am not arguing that all change is necessarily for the good, or that all development goes from simpler to more complex forms every time. In fact, the second law of thermodynamics seems to imply that most things tend to disorder, with only certain pockets "bucking the trend," so to speak, in moving towards more order and complexity.

Where this has happened—that is, where development has inclined toward complexity—we find what astrophysicist Paul Davies has called the "goldilocks effect," whereby the universe appears just right for life to have evolved as it as.[15] If reality is an event that is in relation, then adding to this the concept of change and process leads us to an understanding of the universe (and us) as related events in process. All the previous events that have unfolded (and their interrelations) are moving through time in a process of change.

Whitehead described this process in rather technical terms, but he helps us move beyond thinking of everything in the world as disconnected substances. Whitehead asks us to imagine the present moment as the process of these related events coming together, which he calls concresence. It is when a becoming moment (1) takes in all that the past has to offer it; (2) engages with potentialities offered by God; (3) chooses what to work with from both the past and the immediate potential; in order to (4) create a new future.

Concresence describes the process of change by which creative advance is fundamental to all aspects of life. Jungermann provides a picture of this process and change as fundamental:

Much more complex creativity occurs in life forms. Highly organized life forms, such as humans, are capable of a great deal more enjoyment and creativity than, say, a slime mold. Yet, even at that basic level of life there is rhythmic pulsation of creativity, a search for nourishment, and reproduction. The big bang was a period of magnificent creativity: the space in in our universe was created in an expanding bubble of intense radiation. As the radiation cooled, matter and eventually atoms were formed. Billions of years of creativity followed: galaxies formed, stars ignited. Supernovae produced heavy elements and spewed them into the cosmos. Finally, five billion years ago, our solar system formed and conditions for life as we know it were produced on our planet. The universe is not static but continuously evolving—in the past its composition was very different from its composition at present.[16]

Thinking of time as fundamental can have significant implications. Surprise is fundamental and inherent in the structure of the world. Or, as cosmologist Lee Smolin reminds us, the implication of time being fundamental is that "novelty is real."[17]

Summary

In this chapter, I introduced you to some of the key scientific descriptions of reality that will be useful as a background to our discussion in process theology. For those of you who didn't skip this chapter, I hope that some of the insights above have led you to conclude that reality is fundamentally made up of *interrelated events in a process of continual change*. With these insights in mind, we will now look at several process thinkers who have wrestled with these insights, and we will begin to ask how we might engage with God and faith in light of this.

Chapter 7

Pathways to Process

SOME TRADITIONAL theological trappings are insufficient to help us navigate the questions of suffering, so we need help to get off the omnibus. In this chapter, I will introduce you briefly to six people who will be our guides. All of these people are individuals who I found personally helpful at some difficult and dark times in my own faith journey. Some I am lucky to have gotten to know personally. These six process theologians have unique perspectives that can help reshape our thinking. Virtually all six of them have addressed perspectives that the others have. However, we'll look at just one key idea in process thinking from each of them. This allows us to get a broad introduction to some major process thinkers while at the same time making sure we give sufficient attention to key aspects of process thought. Much of what we cover in this chapter will form the backdrop to our later attempts to rethink God and our involvement in the world. This chapter is also a philosophical and theological response to the chapter that preceded it, which examined the nature of reality. Let us begin with what many would consider the major influence on process thinking and its emergence in the twentieth century: the work of Alfred North Whitehead.

Whitehead and metaphysics

Alfred North Whitehead (1861–1947) was a British mathematician and philosopher who, before turning his hand to philosophy, achieved fame through his work in writing *Principia Mathematica* with his pupil Bertrand Russell. Whitehead was one of the first philosophers to take seriously the numerous discoveries that were taking place in quantum physics and to work out their philosophical implications. He described his approach as speculative philosophy. Simply put, Whitehead argued that we ought to take into account as much data from our experience of the world as we can scientifically (empiricism), and then speculate philosophically or theologically on what this looks like and what it might mean. His famous example is of an airplane that takes off from experience and heads off into the air of speculation, only to return to experience when landing. The speculative philosophical approach is important but must always return to experience to gauge its adequacy. Although from a slightly different angle, this book follows a similar trajectory. I start from my own experience with cancer, begin to engage with philosophical and theological thinking, and hopefully in the end land in real life with plans for action. This is good, practical, theological methodology.

Whitehead's language and philosophy are certainly torturous and not for the fainthearted. This is because he believed we needed new language for the new concepts that were emerging from experience and science. Whitehead's philosophical system, I believe, is consistent with key aspects of the scientific data that describes the nature of reality we looked at previously. Central to Whitehead's thinking is that *the world is a series of interrelated events in the process of becoming*. Reality is made up of what Whitehead calls actual entities, or occasions, or what we are calling events. These actual occasions, or events, can come together to form what Whitehead calls a "society of actual occasions." Hence, a human being would be a complex society of actual occasions that is more than the sum of its parts. More radically, Whitehead believed that God is also an actual entity and, indeed, embodies every actual entity. These actual entities are not simply substances floating in space but are dynamic within themselves and influenced by the past and other current actual entities as they move into the future. I hope I haven't lost you at this point, so try to hang in there. We'll begin to tease this out in the next chapter in a way that might be more accessible.

Whitehead's term for this process, whereby actual occasions move from the past into the future, is called "concresence." I actually think this is an unhelpful term, as it tends to generate the idea of a concrete and a settled substance. This is not what Whitehead was hoping to convey. He wanted to get across the idea that every given moment or event in the universe is influenced by all that has gone before and, through a process of decision, each event shapes its contribution to the future. Now, if all reality is in the process of "concresencing" or "becoming," then this becoming applies to God, human beings, animals, and the atomic realm. The whole of reality (God and universe) is therefore in the process of duration, that is, continuance in time. Again, duration implies that the universe is not static, but is constantly changing and moving. This experience of duration (although relative) is experienced by all reality in what Whitehead refers to as an extensive continuum, which we mentioned previously. It is helpful to keep Bergson's example of the train tracks in mind here. Although both individuals would be moving, they would be moving *together* and connected.

Catherine Keller describes Whitehead's philosophy as one that leads to an "elaborate rethinking of the universe as one immense, living, and open-ended network of spontaneous interactions." The implication for process theology is that God is a living process of interaction. As Keller notes, and we will pick up later, "to discern God in process means to discern at the same time our own participation as social individuals, that is, as individuals who participate in one another and in God."[1]

Whitehead's philosophy helps us to imagine a reality that is a creative process of becoming, where the past flows into the present, and the whole universe is interconnected. In chapter eight we will see how that can shift our understanding of how we imagine God and our interaction with God. At this point, though, we can see that Whitehead offers us a vision of a world that is deeply interconnected, not only within the natural world but to God, as well. Because reality itself is in a constant state of becoming and change, so is God.

One of the first to work out the implications of Whitehead's view of the universe was the philosopher Charles Hartshorne. Thus it is to Hartshorne that we turn next.

Hartshorne and the future

I was on a flight from Melbourne to Sydney when I first read Charles Hartshorne—a book called *A Natural Theology for Our Time*. I confess to having a fear of flying, which means that for most of my life I've done a range of deals with God when I'm on a plane, swinging wildly between fatalism and hoping God would not allow the plane to crash. As I began reading that book, Hartshorne spoke about the fact that God does not know the future. What, I pondered on that very flight, would this mean for my fatalism and for my prayers for God to control my plane?

Charles Hartshorne was Whitehead's research assistant at Harvard and had already worked out some of his own ideas of the existence and nature of God. He became a major exposiler of Whitehead in his many years teaching at the Chicago Divinity

School and, unlike Whitehead, was far more open to and vocal in his affirmation regarding belief in God. In fact, Hartshorne would say the metaphysics requires it. Hartshorne gave me hope in enabling me to think beyond a God that was all-powerful and all-knowing, ideas I believed were inconsistent with a reality filled with suffering and pain, in which cancer was just one such expression. Like Whitehead, Hartshorne affirmed a nonsubstance-based understanding of reality and embraced the reality of process and duration.

Two key texts of Hartshorne are relevant for our discussion, A *Natural Theology for our Time* and *Omnipotence and Other Theological Mistakes*. I will defer the question of omnipotence to when we look at Catherine Keller a little later, but I want at this point to draw out the key insight with regard to omniscience that Hartshorne offers us. Hartshorne rejected aspects of the theological tradition that would place God outside of the flow of time. Rather, he affirms that future events do not exist, not for us and not for God. He notes that:

> God does not already or eternally know what we do tomorrow, for, until we decide, there are no such entities as our tomorrow's decisions.[2]

This is difficult for many religious traditions, and particularly Christian ones, which would like to assert that God exists outside of time and is unchanging. Often the example given in the Christian narrative is of a record. If you were to hold up a record, you could imagine that the hole in the middle symbolizes the beginning of our lives, which start in the center and end on the outer edge of the record. In this image, God represents one who could see all aspects of an individual's life (and all reality, for that matter) from outside of time (like the person holding the record and looking at it).

Hartshorne rejects this understanding of God being outside time and looking at the record. God experiences duration and time with us. The implication is that God experiences each moment as it is happening. God can be surprised by our decisions, and, in fact, we can even change God's mind. Hebrew Bible scholar Robert Gnuse confronts us with that notion when he asks us to come to terms with the reality that much of the Hebrew Bible images of God are deeply consistent with process theology and quite antithetical to many of the doctrines we have inherited. He notes that,

> The God of the biblical text was portrayed in dynamic fashion, as a deity with human emotions whose mind could change. Numerous narratives in the Hebrew Scriptures especially testify to this phenomenon, but it is often the tendency of Jews and Christians to ignore these stories.[3]

This is seen, for example, with the doctrine of omniscience as it is understood within the Christian tradition. Hartshorne reminds us that just because God does not know the future, this does not mean God is not infinitely wise. If God is present everywhere (traditionally understood as omnipresence), then God experiences every event in the universe, both the good and the bad. God feels every moment in a deep, intimate, and interconnected way. God is infinitely wise in that God has always existed and brings the wisdom of the ages to bear on each given moment. Hence, in a very real sense, God does know the best option available to us in each moment. We, however, might not know this. As Monica Coleman said in one of her podcasts, this implies that we might not be cognizant of specific options for our lives that God knows, yet God could still make us aware of what those options are. Something becoming possible (a specific choice or direction), which would never have been possible before (from our limited perspective), is by definition a miracle—the impossible becoming possible. However, this does not guarantee that the specific outcome will be positive for us, even if we are being led and invited by God. Other decisions and events in the world (decisions that cannot be known by God until they have occurred) might thwart the best leading even by God.

If God knows the future, then freedom is an illusion at best, and a mockery at worst. Events would have *already been determined.* With Hartshorne, the future is yet to happen, and hence we are truly free. It also allows prayer to find its rightful place again. Prayer to God, under the scenario where God knows the future already, is really only something that benefits us. It makes us feel better. It can't really effect change. Although prayer is by no means without controversy in process thought, it does re-introduce a dynamic interrelational conversation back into the God-world relationship. Prayer becomes a real conversation with God about the best way forward, about real possibilities. Prayer is also relevant in the sense that God now truly feels with us, *in this given moment,* the agony of any situation and potential decision we face. Hartshorne provides hope, perhaps not in the traditional way of taking comfort in God knowing the future, but certainly hope that God feels every moment with us. God can also provide infinite wisdom to each given moment and is with us from the inside and not from without. It provides hope in that my prayers do have an effect and are not simply an illusion about a future that has already happened. To pray on a plane and encounter God's presence and faithfulness is not a waste of time. Unfortunately, it doesn't mean God *will* or *can* keep the plane in the sky. This raises the question of God's power and the doctrine of omnipotence.

Keller and omnipotence

Although virtually every process theologian has taken aim at the traditional doctrine of omnipotence at some point, it is Catherine Keller who for me highlighted not only the deficiencies of such a doctrine, but also how dangerous it can be for church and society.

This doctrine, perhaps like no other, has proved to be the most troubling when considering the kind of God who would permit evil. In theological terms, this is generally considered the problem of theodicy. We made an initial foray into some of the difficulties with the doctrine of omnipotence in an earlier chapter, so what can Keller add to the discussion here?

Outside of the troubling questions that omnipotence raises for the problem of evil and the nature of a God that would permit suffering, there are at least two key areas that ought to be considered. Firstly, Keller asks us to reject another doctrine that has been associated with the broader concept of omnipotence, namely, the idea of creation out of nothing (*creatio ex nihilo*). Here we have the image of God as someone who literally created the universe out of nothing (no thing). It is a unilateral act of power to bring about a specific outcome. The problem this raises, however, is that if God is all-powerful so as to create the world out of nothing, can't God simply use the same power to intervene now? Keller asks us to reject the notion of creation out of nothing, or creation *ex nihilo*. She rather proposes that we think of creation as creation *ex profundis*. Don't worry too much about the Latin terminology, but try to imagine a potter working with clay that already exists. The clay was always already there for the potter to work with. We can in the same way now imagine God working deeply and profoundly with the world to invite and persuade it towards a specific outcome. I would argue that this image is actually more in line with the Genesis narrative whereby the spirit of God hovers over the deep (chaos) to bring something from it.[4] Here God is *working with and persuading*, rather than intervening directly and coercively.

Keller, in rejecting omnipotence, proposes a deity who is in an interdependent activity of becoming with us,

> Each actuality, divine included, is a process of embodiment contracting in itself the entangled materializations of the universe. The metaphor is of divinity as one who does not

control any creature, even an electron.... Divine agency then does not control the outcome of any becoming, even its own. It *causes* only by calling. It does not coerce, command, or hack its way into the creature.⁵

Related to this, but from a slightly different angle, is the second notion; that is, in traditional theology, God's power is omnipotent throughout—in the beginning, at the creation, and at the end. Accordingly, in the Book of Revelation we find God using violent means to destroy God's enemies to bring about God's desired outcome. But if we reject God's unilateral use of power, then we reject God's use of coercive violence, as well, even for a utopian end. Thus, whether looking backwards to creation or forward to the future, an interventionist God causes us problems. Keller makes the necessary conclusion that "God cannot do it for us" and that

> if we perpetuate a theology of omnipotent control, we can blame all of our failings on God who might have intervened, might have rescued us. The failure might feel like a betrayal. But the betrayal, it seems after all, is our own. And our theology, our God-construct, is complicit.⁶

She asks us to think instead of power as persuasive and not coercive, as a working with rather than a forcing to. Rejecting omnipotence allows us to forgive God, but it further enables us to reject coercive power and to rather think how power can operate persuasively to bring about a desired future. Keller offers a powerful concluding vision and asks us to:

> let the hierarchical universe of unilateral and omnipotent sovereignty fade into a more widely democratic cosmos of unpredictable and uncontrollable—but never unordered—interrelations. God is called upon not as a unilateral superpower but as a relational force, not an omnipotent creator

from nothing, imposing order upon chaos, but the lure to a self-organizing complexity, creating out of the chaos.[7]

Dombrowski and experience

In his last book the renowned neurologist Oliver Sacks challenges us to think about how nonhuman life experiences the world. In a chapter entitled "The Mental Lives of Worms and Plants," Sacks engages with Darwin's insistence that animal and plant life is much closer than we might think. Sacks note that:

> It is fascinating to think of Darwin, Romanes, and other biologists of their time searching for "mind," "mental processes," "intelligence," even "consciousness" in primitive animals like jellyfish, and even in protozoa. A few decades afterwards, radical behaviorism would come to dominate the scene, denying reality to what was not objectively demonstrable, denying in particular any inner processes *between* stimulus and response, deeming these irrelevant or at least beyond the reach of scientific study.[8]

Experience might be further extended even to the quantum realm along with the organic life that Sachs was addressing. This is what we are about to explore with the help of our next guide, Daniel Dombrowski. Dombrowski is a professor of philosophy at Seattle University. He has written extensively on Whitehead, process philosophy, and theology. I have chosen Dombrowski to explain a key feature of process thought that claims all of reality is experiencing, and is not simply static and uninfluenced by what is going on around it.

Out of all the things I chose to introduce you to in process theology, this is the one area I am unsure of. It is particularly complex, and often raises more questions than it answers. It is also at the forefront of broader quests in science and philosophy to understand the origin and nature of consciousness, making much of what I write more speculative than it already is! In the end I decided to include this key feature of process thought, as its implications are important for an ecological ethic and our relatedness to God and to the natural world.

A key feature of Whitehead's understanding of reality is that events, not substances, are primary. These most basic elements of existence are called actual entitites or actual occasions. In process theology, new occasions emerge from the influence of past occasions and from a divine "lure"—a prompting from God. Each becoming occasion decides for itself which of the past feelings and which of the divine offerings it will accept and use in its own self-formation. It then becomes part of the influx of past occasions influencing a new event.

Larger aspects of reality, such as a tree or a rock, are what Whitehead calls "societies of actual occasions." This does not mean that a rock is alive, but it does mean that it is dynamic. In aggregates, such as rocks and chairs, actual entities are combined in such a way that the object is not living, but the movement of electrons and photons is discernible at a quantum level. It is unsurprising that the physicist Carlo Rovelli would want to call a rock an "event."[9]

As we move beyond rocks to more complex "societies," things change. As more complex connections take place up the evolutionary tree, for example, one can imagine the building blocks of consciousness taking place. This is a controversial topic, but consider the following atheist philosophers when exploring the possibility that, even at a basic level, consciousness or feeling can be fundamental.

Astrophysicist Paul Davies argues that the two greatest mysteries we face are why the universe seems fine-tuned for life and why human beings are conscious.[10] Ultimately, for Davies (who is neither a Christian nor a theist in the classical sense), this means that there must be some kind of mind behind the universe as it is.[11] The problem of consciousness that Davies raises continues to plague both scientists and philosophers alike. For David Chalmers, the hard problem of consciousness has to do with why we experience the world at all. The soft problem of consciousness deals simply with how consciousness functions. Some proposals suggest that consciousness is a problem too hard to solve,[12] or that it is simply an epiphenomenon[13]—in other words, just something that happens to the mind, a byproduct. Thomas Nagel argues that those kinds of reductionist explanations are not supported by the scientific evidence. He doesn't suggest what the answer is, but proposes something not dissimilar to the implications of Whitehead's metaphysics.

> My preference for an immanent, natural explanation is congruent with my atheism. But even a theist who believes God is ultimately responsible for the appearance of conscious life could maintain that this happens as part of a natural order that is created by God, but that it does not require further divine intervention. A theist not committed to dualism in the philosophy of mind could suppose that the natural possibility of conscious organisms resides already in the character of the elements out of which those organisms are composed, perhaps supplemented by laws of psychophysical emergence.[14]

At risk of over quoting, at this point I give you Chalmers' call for a reevaluation of consciousness in relation to nature:

> Consciousness fits uneasily into our conception of the natural world. On the most common conception of nature, the natural world is the physical world. But on the most common conception of consciousness, it is not easy to see how it could be part of the physical world. So it seems that to find a place for consciousness within the natural order,

we must either revise our conception of consciousness or revise our conception of nature.[15]

As you might imagine, I propose we reconceive our conception of nature, and I suggest that process thinking gives us just the language to begin thinking about this in the right way.

Dombrowski himself references Chalmers as someone in the philosophical tradition who has argued that experience might be fundamental to reality. Dombrowski builds on this in his engagement with Griffin and Hartshorne. He uses the terminology of actual occasions (Whitehead's term) to describe this fundamental aspect of reality.

Dombrowski says that each actual occasion is an experiencing occasion because it influences, and is influenced by, others.[16] Dombrowski summarizes how experience, at a very basic level, takes form and shape in larger wholes (societies of actual occasions):

> Only some wholes bring together the experiences of the parts into experience as an integral individual. In fact, it is most notably animals, including human animals, with central nervous systems that do so.... Other wholes—like insentient rocks and trees and automobiles—are mere aggregates, even if there is experience in their subatomic or cellular parts.[17]

Thus Dombrowski rejects claims that nature is *totally* insentient, and he looks at cell theory and subatomic science to demonstrate this. Rather, nature is everywhere active. The Celtic mystic John O'Donohue asks us to remind ourselves of this every time we walk out of our homes in the morning, that everything around us is alive.[18] It's something I try to do each day as I open my door before I get in my car to head to work. Everything is alive; we are not alone!

The technical term that Dombrowski uses to describe this all-experiencing reality is *panexperientialism* or *panpsychicism*. Biologically, as science continues to progress, we are finding more studies that support intelligence and consciousness in more than human life. Even bacteria, it is now being claimed, has some sense of memory.[19] Recent studies involving how trees feel and communicate with one another give further evidence of this, along with animal studies involving octopi and dolphins.[20]

The fact that all of life is experiencing and feeling (although not necessarily conscious like we are) will prove important when we look at panentheism and emergence next. It is crucial, however, that Dombrowski's more general argument from Whitehead—that all of reality is experiencing and feeling—should cause us to have a deeper reverence and respect for life. The French philosopher Didier Debaise argues that this insight by Whitehead should remind us that:

> The sense of value, of importance, and of purpose ... are to be found everywhere, from the most elementary forms of life of microorganisms to reflective consciousness.[21]

I suspect that I might not be fully able to convince you of the fact that all of reality is "experiencing" in some way. It is impossible, though, to give a full account of process thinking without paying attention to one of its central convictions. The fact that all of reality is experiencing in some way should generate awe and wonder towards creation. This should hopefully challenge our actions towards the environment at the same time. But in terms of process theology, it should remind us of our interconnectedness to the rest of the planet. It also forms the important link in our relationship to and engagement with God, for God is also experiencing all aspects of a universe that is also experiencing itself. Panexperientialism can be affirmed by those who do not believe in God.

Panexperientialism provides the necessary building blocks for understanding *panenetheism*, to which we now turn. If everything can experience, then everything can potentially experience God, and God can experience everything.

Griffin and panentheism

As a young Christian I remember only three options: "atheism," "theism," and "pantheism." Pantheism was seen as everything to do with Eastern religions and something to be avoided at all costs. "Panentheism" was never presented as an option I could even consider. In a later chapter I will explore the implications of panentheism for how we think about the world and God. To help us frame that later discussion, I turn first to panentheism as it is understood by process theologian David Ray Griffin. Griffin has, of course, like the others in this chapter, addressed the nature of metaphysics, omniscience, and omnipotence, as well as divine action.

At the risk of radically oversimplifying, but with the potential benefit of clarity, I will outline the three terms above in order to help us understand the God-world relationship, and panentheism in particular.

> Although people have often been led to believe that they must choose from among only three options—traditional theism, pantheism, and atheism—there is a fully distinct fourth alternative, panentheism, which an increasing number of thinkers are finding more satisfactory.[22]

Certain aspects of traditional theism can be articulated as the belief that God and the world are radically distinct. God is outside of time and the universe is inside of time. God then needs to enter into the world from the outside to engage with the universe. Atheism would hold that the universe (or multiverse) is all there is, and that there is no such thing as a God. Pantheism, often associated with Eastern religions, holds that the universe is God, and that God is not personal in any sense. Panentheism rejects all three of these alternatives and offers an alternate vision.

According to process panentheism, God is *essentially* the

soul of the universe: Although God is distinct from the universe, God's relation to it belongs to the divine essence.[23]

Griffin argues that much of the doctrinal content of omnipotence, omniscience, and divine causation emerge from the traditional theistic perspective. He describes the atheistic view as naturalistic, and the traditional theistic view as supernatural. These categories begin to break down with a panentheistic perspective, as we will soon see.

A panentheistic approach still affirms the omnipresent nature of God (the only "omni" I'm willing to keep on the omnibus!), where God and the universe are interwoven and interconnected, yet distinct. God is not outside creation, and creation is not outside of God. This brings new meaning to the biblical injunction that in "God we live and move and have our being."[24] It was Hegel who noted that it would not make sense to have God (the infinite) outside of creation (the finite), as logically this would mean God would not be truly infinite.[25]

The benefits of thinking panentheistically are numerous. For one, God is never far away from us, but is ever present in our suffering and pain.[26] Further to this, we can begin to think about the re-enchantment of nature.[27] Traditional animistic societies believed that spirits were present at certain locations, such as special hedge groves or trees. Early missionaries rejected this and sought to stamp out these practices. By thinking panentheistically we can now think of the Earth and the environment as literally charged with the presence of God. If we combine this with Dombrowski's reminder that all of creation (and particularly organic life) is in certain ways experiencing, we can then begin to generate an ecological ethic that sees creation both as alive and enchanted. This panentheistic perspective, Griffin reminds us, will influence how we think about both divine causation and religious experience.[28] It is with the help of Philip Clayton that we now briefly turn to address divine causation and religious experience from a process perspective.

Clayton and emergence

Philip Clayton is indebted to process thinking, but in some ways departs from many of the traditional assumptions of process thought. Alongside his engagement with process theology, Clayton studied under the well-known German theologian Wolfhart Pannenberg. Clayton is involved in the faith and science dialogue, and is editor of the *Oxford Handbook of Religion and Science*.[29] Clayton offers some important insights that I believe will prove helpful at a later point in our discussion.

Clayton is a strong proponent of panentheism, whereby God and world are interconnected yet distinct. This is implied in Whitehead's metaphysics and his description of reality, whereby God and the world are within each other, interconnected, related, mutually influencing each other in a joint process of becoming and duration. Clayton provides a unique insight in exploring the process of "emergence" within creation. This debate has implications for freedom and causation more generally, but for our purpose Clayton asks us to accept the scientific story of emergence and the four major transitions in the natural world. They are as follows:

1. Quantum physics to macro physical systems and chemistry;
2. Chemistry to complex biological organisms and ecosystems;
3. The brain and central nervous system to the phenomena of consciousness or "mind"; and
4. The emergence of spirit within the natural order, including the questions of its ultimate nature and origin.[30]

Clayton has spent significant time examining the scientific literature on emergence[31] and articulating the different views within the scientific community. Clayton argues for what is known as strong emergence, where stages that are more complex in evolution (say, a multicellular organism) can have downward causation and influence the parts of which is it composed (the various individual cells that make up a multicellular organism). He applies this principle all the way up the chain of evolution. Mind, or Spirit, can now have downward causation on the body from which it has emerged. He speculates that Mind and Spirit can now become the locus and space whereby engagement with the reality of God might take place. This is not to discount the rest of creation as it is found within God, per Griffin, but Clayton believes that something unique is now possible with humans.

Clayton is one who does not believe that God can (or should) break the physical laws of nature in order to intervene in creation. He believes that even if God could, God shouldn't, as this would raise significant ethical (and theodicy) challenges about why God would intervene in one situation of life and not another.[32] With the emergence of mind, however, interaction and communication with God that does not require the breaking of physical laws could take place. He believes that God's influence on the world, taking place at the level of the mind, is persuasive (not coercive). For God to intervene in an event, there must be a response from the creature. An extended quote below from Clayton is included because it sums up crucial implications of much of the discussion to date around process theology, but also forms the basis of much that follows in this book. With regards to divine action, Clayton notes the following:

> Though it limits the efficacy of the divine will in the world, I nonetheless believe that this position is sufficient to sustain a viable and scientifically acceptable form of theism for today's world.
>
> Consequently, theists do not need to imagine that God brings about human actions or physical events by divine fiat alone. Divine causality is better understood as a form

of causal influence that prepares and persuades. On the one hand, this result makes it much more difficult to conceive a divine influence on rocks or other purely physical systems apart from the laws and initial conditions established by God at creation. On the other hand, it does continue to ascribe to God a crucial and causal role in "luring" humanity (and, for all we know, perhaps other biological agents as well) and in influencing the interpersonal, moral, intellectual, and aesthetic dimensions of human personhood. The resulting position emphasizes a genuine openness in history.[33]

As I've tried to take the work of Clayton seriously, I've concluded that God cannot intervene physically in the world, and neither can God force propositional content at the level of the mind. Rather, it is perhaps a question of certain individuals being able to "tune in" to the right "frequency" for communication to be experienced. I am aware that this raises enormous difficulties in other areas that will need to be considered with regard to an individual's receptive abilities, and what this means for faith and practice. Clayton argues that the openness of individuals to this divine engagement could potentially be advanced by meditative and spiritual practices. It could even be that there is an "openness" to a transcendent mind and spirit that would be required for this to take place. Our own selfish ambitions and various other dynamics could block this encounter and engagement from happening. Cultural and conceptual resources could further influence the nature of this divine communication.

> One could imagine a specific constellation of factors that reduced a person's receptivity to a minimum, and one can formulate factors that would presumably make one maximally responsive to divine leading. All of these factors taken together would have an impact on the degree of clarity with which the communication might take place.[34]

Although God as spirit is involved in all aspects of reality (as Dombrowski reminds us), the emergence of mind enables us to be involved with the Spirit in ways that have not been possible before. We will pick up on some of this in the last chapter. As someone who emerged from within the Pentecostal-Charismatic tradition, I found Clayton particularly helpful in reconceiving (returning?) in some ways to the possibility of encounter with the divine.

Summary

In this chapter I have introduced you to some of the central themes of process theology that will be worked out in the pages to come. There are many other process thinkers that I could have included here, as well as other aspects of process theology that people might feel I neglected. What I have tried to do is include those features that I believe are central, as well as those that have been most helpful (and hopeful) in my rethinking about God and God's relationship with the world.

Whitehead reminds us of the reality that everything is changing in a multiplicity of becoming. Hartshorne challenges us with the implication that God does not know exactly what the future will look like, which is a radical re-visioning of traditional omniscience. Keller builds on this by arguing that omnipotence is not plausible in process thinking, and that God is not all powerful, but rather invites us towards a preferred future. This inviting takes place against the background of affirming our interconnectedness to all of experiencing reality. This all-experiencing reality is something that we experience with and in God, which Griffin articulated as panentheism; all is in God, and God is in all, but God is not limited to all. In Clayton's description of emergence, life flows from these interrelations and offers possibilities for our religious experience and encounters with God.

Chapter 8

Can the Real God Please Stand Up?

Process philosophy has always taken God and the world seriously. If what I have been suggesting is true, and the universe we inhabit is always changing, always in process and, indeed, an interconnected event, then what does this mean for our understanding of God? Having discussed the nature of reality and covered some of the key ideas and thinkers in process theology, we can continue with some of the fundamental questions that cancer raised for me in relation to my faith. Perhaps these are questions you have asked yourself.

Where is God?

Traditional theology generally has two ideas of where God is and how God is related to us. As we have seen, the dominant approach has been to think of God as largely outside of time and disconnected from the universe. God then chooses at different points to enter the world and engage with it. Here, the world is radically separate from and not connected to God. God is infinite and the world is finite.

Another way of conceiving this is that God and the world are collapsed into one, known as the pantheistic (not panentheistic) understanding of reality mentioned earlier. God is the world, and the world is God.

A view that is coming into more prominence in certain theological circles today, and across faith traditions, is the view known as *panentheism,* which Griffin helped to articulate earlier. In this view, God is in the world (but not limited to the world), and the world is within God. They are distinct entities, yet are metaphysically and literally connected. This is the view mostly endorsed by process theologians.[1]

If the world is in God and God is in the world, then God is everywhere and in everything. A good example of this is the way Peter Singer describes panentheism in his discussion of Hegel.[2] Singer asks us to imagine the interconnection in a way that is similar to how we inhabit our bodies. We know that our bodies are part of who we are, and yet we have minds that appear in some way as being distinct from our bodies. In the same way, we can imagine God as the mind of the universe, and the universe as God's body. I am aware of the difficulties of this metaphor which, like all good metaphors, breaks down at some point, and I do not want to downplay the complex debates around the mind-body problem; nevertheless, I find this image useful.

Thinking of God's presence in a panentheistic sense is radical, implying that God alone is aware of everything that goes on in the universe. The good, the bad, and the ugly. Another way of saying this, which Whitehead articulated, is that "God is the great companion—the fellow-sufferer who understands."[3] God really has no way to escape the world's suffering, as God is always present. God cannot escape the brutality of the world, even though we might be able to at certain points.

So, in answer to the question, "Where is God?" we answer that God is everywhere, all of the time, present to all. All is in God and God is in all. This leads to the next key insight generated by the question as to the nature of change in the divine.

Does God change?

One of the key insights of process thinking is that God is subject to influence and change. This means that God can change God's mind, as we see at times in the Hebrew Bible, for example. Due to the interconnected nature of reality and the close God-world connection described by panentheism, God feels what we feel and is moved and influenced by that in the process. I am also open to the potential that God develops in moral capacity over time. I believe that God could be influenced by our moral imagination, as much as we might be influenced by God's.

One of the key implications of this, which we discussed earlier, is that prayer really does matter. We converse with God about real possibilities and discuss real options. This leads me to one of the more robust insights of process theology. Prayer, traditionally understood, had always appeared contradictory to me. If God is outside of time, as well as knowing the future, then, really, prayer is something that might make me feel better but is unlikely to change God, God's mind, or the situation. God would already know the decision we would make. However, if prayer is to have any sense of meaning, it is best understood when God does not know the future.

What does God know?

Omniscience is the word that religions have often used to describe God's all-knowing power—one of the "omnis" rejected by Hartstorne, as noted in the last chapter. The word itself often implies that not only does God know all there is to know right now (which we've affirmed), but also all that is to come (which I can't affirm). I have already questioned this at numerous points, particularly in my discussion of how God became a problem. In that chapter the context of the discussion was of a God who would knowingly create a world with so much suffering, and I implicated God as partly responsible for death and suffering. If God is morally evolving in some way, then this might also help us understand God's original decision. This is the point where I believe we need to offer forgiveness to God, for God must have known that some form of suffering would take place. Nevertheless, God could not have foreseen the amount of suffering that would unfold.

There are implications for this in our day-to-day living and the decisions we make regarding our future. Process theology affirms that God is in one sense eternal, but in another sense subject to the reality of time and duration.[4] That is, God is also in process, and therefore God's future is also open. Several powerful results follow from this idea. Firstly, God does not know what decision you will make with regard to your situation. You are truly free to make your own choices. Secondly, God can see a multitude of potential futures for your life due to God's supreme wisdom and knowledge of who you are and the world you inhabit. Thirdly, God might have a preferred path through all those possible options, one that might still result in an unfortunate outcome, even if you follow God's lead. Prayer makes an important contribution here, too. Prayer is now a conversation that involves a real and meaningful communication about a range of possible choices and outcomes.

If the future has not yet happened, then that future has not happened for God, either. God is then to some extent surprised by the decisions we make and does not know them in advance. God is all-knowing, though, in the sense that at any given moment, due to the fact that God is present everywhere and everything is related, God would know all. Affirming God as supremely wise would certainly be true. God, with the wisdom of the past and the knowledge of everything knowable, can invite us to a future that God desires not only for ourselves but also for the planet. This, of course, has ramifications for the question of omnipotence. If God does not know the future and cannot prevent certain outcomes, then by definition God would not be all-powerful. Yet the fact that God is supremely wise does allow God to offer to the planet, and to us as individuals, the potential futures that God would deem best according to that wisdom.

What can God do?

A central insight of process thinking is that God is not an all-powerful being that can tinker with the universe and its laws at will. God rather invites us to participate in the world and in each new situation in a way that is best for that current moment and any impasse it might be confronting. That is, God can only work with what God has. Two very different examples of this can be given to illustrate this point.

At a time in the universe where atoms had not combined to form molecules, God could not magically offer a route for atoms to become cells. One of the possible routes God could take, however, is for atoms to combine to form molecules, becoming cells only in some distant future. The same applies to us as human beings who have been born, and developed over time, with certain talents for specific tasks and skills. God might suggest an opportunity that is in line with my skills and talents, but could not simply manufacture talents and situations for me to move into. God can only suggest possibilities and options from those that present themselves and that are realistic. What God can do is invite us toward situations and directions that are available and possible, based on our past history, that we might not be aware of.

Perhaps through prayer we could become more aware of these opportunities, or find ways to handle certain situations, that we might not have known were possible beforehand. What might have been impossible to know without God's wisdom can, through prayer, become possible. By some accounts the impossible becoming possible is the definition of a miracle. Much of this requires us doing our best in our spiritual formation to to learn how to engage with God so we can become aware of these possibilities.

A God that has all power and doesn't act to reduce the suffering of people seems desperately cruel. Often Christians have spoken about praying for a car park, or some other trivial thing in their lives. They claim that God then gave them a parking place, or an iPad, or something else. I would find a God who did this to be morally reprehensible. Hopefully, God would be willing to communicate with us about human trafficking in various parts of the world. If your God gives you a parking place and doesn't help these young girls, I suggest finding another God. I know that the previous sentences are particularly strong language, but we need to sit with that kind of thought to realize some of the misconceptions that circulate regarding prayer.

More controversially, I don't believe God has the power to actively intervene in the world even once (as Clayton suggested). If God has the power to intervene but does not, even one intervention would morally imply that God should come to the aid of others.[5] If God chooses to heal one person of cancer and not another, we need to ask why. Appealing to mystery is not an answer but a cop out. Saying that God does only certain things to advance God's overall cause in the world is simply evangelical gymnastics. This God appears to me to be partial in allowing needless suffering to achieve a certain agenda. If such a God exists, I cannot worship this God.

In a panentheistic, interconnected, changing, processive, and eventful world, the interaction between God and the universe might take many shapes and forms (along with different ethical requirements), many of which we might not know. The various religious and nonreligious traditions of the world could point to different ways of doing this, either passive or active. I would argue that many of the institutions around the world (both governmental and religious) might have the potential to embody the values and ethics God would want for the world (or they have at some point in the past). Of course, these institutions are always open to revision as even God's understanding might shift and change, needing novel ways of being lived out and embodied in the world. Some of these changes we will discuss in the next chapter, climate change being one of them.

My current view is that there are certain ways of being with God and ways of behaving in the world that make us more susceptible to the experience of God, similar to tuning into a radio frequency. Unfortunately, this illustration breaks down because I do not believe God reveals content in words. Could we become infused with the values that God would want us to have to make the right choices? I realize for many of us this will be an inadequate conception of the communication between ourselves and God, leaving more questions than answers.

I, for one, do not believe God restrains Godself for moral or other reasons. The suffering is too great across the animal and human world for this to make sense. Speculatively, I concur with the thought experiment that Hans Jonas spoke about in *God after Auschwitz*.

In that article Jonas imagines a scenario whereby God creates a universe in which God is embodied in that universe. In this desire of God's to take form in matter (yet always in a panentheistic sense) God must lay aside all power to create the universe. God then risks not only the future of the universe, but God's own future, too. What if creation does not respond to the divine invitation to complexity and development? What would this mean for God?

In this thought experiment, God does not have hands and feet, but the universe (in response to God's lures and invitations), becomes God's hands and feet. God's "power" here is not coercive but persuasive. Ultimately, though, God cannot force the situation, only stay eternally committed to each present moment and person. Because God's power is not coercive or interventionist, this means that often times the only options available might be equally distressing. In this scenario, the most we can hope for is the divine presence of love to be present with us.

I quote the story Jonas offers at length because I believe it captures wonderfully so many aspects of process thinking. It also allows us the opportunity to see the importance of our acts and deeds in the world.

> In the beginning, for unknowable reasons, the ground of being, or the divine, chose to give itself over to the chance and risk and endless variety of becoming. And wholly so: entering into the adventure of space and time, the deity held back nothing of itself—no uncommitted or unimpaired part remained to direct, correct, and ultimately guarantee the roundabout working out of its destiny in the creation. On this unconditional immanence the modern temper insists. It is its courage or despair, in any case its bitter honesty, to take our being-in-the-world seriously: to view the world as left to itself, its laws as brooking no interference, and the rigour of our belonging to it as not softened by an extramundane providence. Our myth demands the same for God's being-in-the-world. Not, however, in the sense of a pantheistic immanence.... But rather, in order that the world might be, and be for itself, God renounced his own being, divesting himself of his deity—to receive it back from the Odyssey of time laden with the chance harvest of unforeseeable temporal experience; transfigured,

or possibly even disfigured, by it. In such self-forfeiture of divine integrity for the sake of an unprejudiced becoming, no other foreknowledge can be admitted than that of *possibilities* which cosmic being offers in its own terms. To these conditions God committed his cause, effacing himself for the sake of the world.[6]

So much of this myth is similar to process theology and its understanding of God: (1) God's foreknowledge is rejected; (2) God is limited by reality itself; (3) God is present in everything; (4) God can change, can be influenced by God's engagement with the world; (5) God is not omnipotent. As Jonas writes, this surely is the only kind of God we can worship post-Auschwitz. When I first read Jonas' myth, I felt instantly that this was a God I could relate to and with whom I would want to participate in generating a more hopeful, just, and merciful world.

The beautiful side of all this is that God's all-knowing wisdom, and God's ever-present and unwavering commitment to the best possible outcome, allows us to respond in ways that could bring about significant goodness and peace in the world.

In the next section, I will highlight some practical perspectives that I believe God might be inviting us to consider in our current context. I will also ask us to draw close to God (despite complexities and unanswered questions) to figure out our unique part in God's dream for the world. This might result in us wanting to consider embracing and risking an adventure with the Divine to generate a happier and healthier world. It might challenge us to participate in the big challenges facing our planet, without the guarantee of a settled outcome. After forgiving God, we can truly embrace a risky adventure with the Divine. But before we end this chapter, I want to name some of the implications regarding the kind of God that emerges from process theology, or what God is like. This will prove vital for making the next move; namely, asking what kind of world we would like, and how we would participate with God in bringing it about.

What is God like?

Podcaster and theologian Tripp Fuller often says that one's view of God should at least be as nice as Jesus. I agree that this is certainly not a bad place to start. But I would approach this question on the basis of the discussion we've had to date. What kind of God is implied by infinite wisdom, presence in everything, and faithfulness to each new moment and event? What kind of God is implied by the reality that God changes and is part of a process of becoming?

If God's existence is eternal, and all of reality is located within God and God within reality, we are confronted with a God that is infinitely wise. Combined with a God that changes and develops, we have a God who has benefited from the infinite wisdom of the ages. This God now offers God's wisdom to each moment of existence towards a desired future reality. A God who changes also implies that this God is open, open to the world and to influence. This means that we have the opportunity to influence God through our prayers and actions. As difficult as this is to hear, we can change God. This kind of God is one in which we can therefore truly say we have the potential for a mutual relationship.

In being everywhere present, God also suffers. For many, but sadly not all of us, we can attempt to remove ourselves from some of the horrors of the world. Not so for God. God has nowhere to go to get away. Jürgen Moltmann retells Elie Wiesel's story of the young boy in the concentration camp. He was being hanged by the Nazi's, and the rest of the inmates were forced to watch the execution. The hanging was proving unsuccessful, though, and the child suffered for long minutes before he died. One of those watching called out, "Where is God?" Another inmate answered, "There hanging."[7] This is a horrible story, but Moltmann was asking us to consider a God that suffers with us, or as Whitehead says, "A fellow sufferer who understands." God comes face to face with all horrors, and therefore God is moved. God gets angry, sad, and dare I say depressed. Is this a God we can relate to and engage with? I hope so.

This God is not all-powerful, but can only invite us towards a preferred future. This means that the implications of being an omnipotent God (where God is neglectful or sadistic) falls by the wayside. Rather, the picture emerges of a God who is faithful to each and every moment. No matter the outcome of the decisions we make, God will continue to be present and offer wisdom to the next moment of decision-making. This is not a God who breaks the rules of the physical universe, but a God who works within the structure of reality—that is, non-supernaturally—to generate a more just and positive form of living and life.

Summary

So much of what I have been writing in this chapter is about the kind of God I feel I can worship. If you have followed my journey so far, hopefully you can see how my experience of cancer led me to question my traditional assumptions about God and God's involvement in the world. This opened me up to process theology, which has been an attempt to respond to many of the scientific conceptions about how the world is structured. We've discovered that this reality is a process of interrelated events, always changing. Whitehead then offers us a philosophical vision in light of this structure of reality. Process theology works out the implications of this by challenging omnipotence, omniscience, and the way the world is related to God. This opens us up to a different vision of God and how we might relate to God and the world. In the next chapter I would like to tentatively explore with you how I have tried, and am trying, to work out the implications of this in my own life. It raises the question of whether God has a dream for the world and how we might want to participate with God in the risky adventure of creating a more just, merciful, and sustainable world..

Chapter 9

What Should We Be Doing? Joining the Adventure

It was Marcus Borg who introduced me to the concept of God having a dream for the world. It appeared in his book *The God We Never Knew.* Borg described it as follows:

> the dream of God is a social and political vision of a world of justice and peace in which human beings do not hurt or destroy, oppress or exploit one another. It is the dream expressed with many images and by many voices in the Bible . . .
>
> The dream of God is a vision of *shalom*, a rich Hebrew word often translated as "peace" but meaning much more than the absence of war. It means well-being in a comprehensive sense. It includes freedom from negatives such as oppression, anxiety, and fear, as well as the presence of positives such as health, prosperity, and security. *Shalom* thus includes a social vision: the dream of a world in which such well-being belongs to everybody.[1]

Does God have a dream for the world?

Some people find the idea of God having a dream for the world a cheesy concept, or perhaps too loose. Chapter 21 in the book of Revelation offers us an image of the kind of world that we might aspire to in the reduction of suffering and pain.[2] In its closing chapters Revelation speaks of a new heaven and a new earth, where there are no more tears. So much has been written about Jesus' message regarding the Kingdom of God as something that would happen here on Earth, and not in some far off distant galaxy with the resultant end to the space-time universe.[3] I won't recount all those discussions here. Suffice it to say that recapturing the vision of Jesus as outlined in the Beatitudes would go some way in crafting a vision for what God's dream for the world might look like. Recovering the Hebraic prophetic tradition in turn may provide significant imaginative resources for how we treat the poor and the environment. The same could be said for many other religious and nonreligious traditions and their contribution to crafting a hopeful vision for our future.

My conviction is that God does have a dream for the world that can be found in the best of what these various traditions offer. For many Christians, though, their vision of the future is captured by the idea of Jesus returning on a white horse at some future date in history. But Jesus restoring the world to its former glory, one in which there is no more conflict or pain, can prove problematic. At a base level, there was no original perfect order in the first place.

There has been a strong move amongst certain Christians to emphasize the importance of stewarding the environment and getting involved in social issues. This is important, but it has the potential to lose its motivating force with the "get out of jail free card" where God returns to intervene and fix things in the future, regardless of how bad things have gotten. A process understanding reminds us that God cannot intervene to fix things, and God must rely on our responsiveness to the divine invitation concerning a preferred future. In the same way, we must rely on God's continual faithfulness to each new situation and God's invitation towards the best possible outcome. Ultimately, though, we cannot eliminate the potential risk that we might destroy the planet. This makes even more pressing both our efforts to participate in the world and its issues, and our need to understand and articulate God's preferred future.

In this chapter I will attempt to describe what I believe are some of the most important challenges we face as a planet, along with ways to respond to them. I won't address all of the challenges, and you might disagree with my approach, too. I certainly don't claim to have all the answers, but rather than being overwhelmed by the enormity of the problem, I have always sought small ways I might make a difference.

Global crisis and disorder

One of the more difficult challenges that process theology poses for traditional Christian thought is that it does not accept Jesus returning on a white horse to save us, literally or metaphorically. This is in contrast with process theology's cousin, open theism, which still allows for a decisive interventionist event at the end to bring all things together.[4] This was the most difficult thought for me to accept in my first encounter with process theology, when I read John Cobb and David Ray Griffin's introduction to process theology. For process theology, reality by nature implies risk, and we are on an adventure. The adventure is not preordained or already known to God. It needs to be lived and worked out. Sadly, as a species we *can* actually destroy ourselves, along with the planet. As much as God will continue to invite us into a desired future, God will not, and cannot, coerce us into that future.

The original title for Brian McLaren's book *The Secret Message of Jesus* was called *Jesus and the Suicide Machine*. The original title has stuck with me because it reflects so accurately our current reality as *Homo sapiens* on this planet. Earth is on an incredibly self-destructive path due to human beings. The recent bestseller *Sapiens* by Yuval Hariri charted this maniacal path we have been travelling since our emergence in Africa.[5] It is certainly not only since the advent of modern warfare and the Industrial Revolution that our destructive tendencies have been at play. In this section I hope to demonstrate how a process understanding of reality can help us understand the seriousness of our task, but also the potential for hope and real change as we partner with God's dream for the world.

The impending doom of planet Earth

Climate change is a deeply polarizing issue in the U.S.[6] Christians are also divided on climate but tend to back the conservative positions (I am not assuming that all conservative views are wrong). The difficulty with climate change is that some attribute its effects to other things. We can understand the effects of pollution in our creeks, and we can make the obvious connection between cause and effects. It is more difficult, although not impossible, with climate change. Climate skeptics retort that climate change has always happened and is always happening, and this is true. What is often overlooked, though, is that the amount of carbon we are emitting into the atmosphere is way above historical emissions.[7] The scientific community is unanimous in its assessment that human beings are contributing decisively to this increase in carbon emissions.[8] One of the difficulties in addressing these issues is that it is very hard for us as a species to make sacrifices for future generations, particularly when we might not see the benefit ourselves. In terms of evolution, we often make short-term decisions based on imminent survival. One could, however, make a strong evolutionary argument that if we don't do something about climate change our offspring will have no place to live and our "line" will die out. Brian McLaren has often reminded Christians that they can fuss over gay marriage as the most important issue if they like, but if the climate is not addressed there will be no planet for us to live on, gay or straight or otherwise.

The issue of climate change is the most serious existential threat we have faced as a species. Even if you feel the whole climate change concept is a conspiracy concocted by left wing liberals, I would ask you to consider the very obvious impact we as a species are having on our environment and the food chain. Regardless of climate change, these are certainly issues we should all be engaged in.

It's difficult to know which global policies and strategies are best to tackle the issue of climate change. This is why it's important to trust the climate scientists. What I offer is rather a small attempt to describe ways that I have found to address climate change and, by implication, participate in God's dream for the world. But first I want to stress the importance for Christians to stay engaged in social issues more generally, and the importance of community groups as vehicles for making God's dream for the world possible.

Staying engaged

Following the shock election of Donald Trump in the 2016 American election, it was easy for many people to embrace a sense of despair. Brexit appeared to further cement the rise of a nationalist politics that had been taking root for some time in many parts of the world. It's easy to dismiss nationalism as a purely negative phenomenon, as in the case of such populist movements as have arisen in Italy and Austria. There are legitimate nationalist movements, though, such as those that have arisen in the quest for Catalonian independence. It is not so easy to make the call on which movement is "in the right" in its quest to cement its nationalist identity. What is unfortunate in many of these quests is the fear-based proposals that seek to exclude the other and denigrate human rights. Sadly, nationalist politics is often tinged with a conservative edge that seeks to reject the reality of climate change and is antagonistic towards other religions, sexes, minorities, and different cultures. Tragically, those aligned with the Christian message often walk hand in hand with those who tout these policies and who thereby inflame the rhetoric.[9] This is often at the expense of the core ideas of Christianity, whereby all are created in the image of God. The radical edge of the prophetic tradition and the counter-cultural and counter-imperial message of Jesus and the kingdom are blunted.

In the current context it might be tempting for Christians to withdraw completely from seeking to bring about change in the world and its structures. This is not a uniquely Christian problem, but perhaps a decidedly human one. Evolutionarily we are prone to fight or flight when danger is imminent. When the world is in such turmoil, it is easy to simply check out of taking responsibility for what is going on. It is not difficult to reject the call to participate in alleviating the sufferings and structural injustices that we may come across. This is particularly so if we are well fed and have good jobs.

One of the key texts I read when I was a young theology student was a small book on Christian mission in South Africa. The lesson the text brought home for me is that being ambivalent is simply an endorsement of the status quo.[10] By not choosing a side (say on racism/slavery) you by default endorse the current system. And for many of us these are systems that we obviously benefit from. Those who despair of the political process often attempt to embody their hopes for change in their own lives or in their communities. This is certainly moving in the right direction. We shouldn't see political and structural change as something that is in opposition to personal and communal activism. This is a false dichotomy. It was Gandhi who said change starts with the individual, although even this is a massive oversimplification. Communal and structural change can bring about different ways of thinking, believing, and behaving in individuals that would not have happened if the change had not taken place. When change is not possible politically, or at least not immediately possible, we can elicit change through the communities we are part of.

Communities and zones of resistance

One of the most insightful books I have read on the power of communities to bring about change is Rodney Stark's *The Rise of Christianity*. Stark undertook a sociological analysis of reasons why Christianity spread throughout the Roman Empire. Among the many reasons Stark discusses:

(1) the early Christians took a progressive attitude toward the role of woman and slaves, both considered minority groups in the Roman Empire;

(2) Christians looked after the weak and the poor when many in Roman society would not (this is most notably seen in the challenge of the Roman emperor Julian who noted that the Christians looked after not only their poor, but ours as well!).[11]

The communities that Christians formed were both inclusive and caring, embodying their faith in the practices and rituals that would help foster this. Christian communion was originally a love feast whereby those in the community would bring food and wine to share with each other, not the individual wafer and grape juice used by many today.[12]

These communities of hope and justice were so transformative that Christianity soon spread throughout the Roman Empire. By the time Constantine legalized Christianity he was simply endorsing a fact: Christianity had become a dominant religion within the empire. Can our communities be as transformative today?

Peter Rollins believes that communities can be transformative.

He is a theologian who has engaged with the Christian tradition from a psychoanalytical perspective, offering new ways of imaginative living in our own lives and the world. Rollins was quick to point out the potential for communities to bring change following the election of Donald Trump. Rollins defined Zones of Resistance as communities that practice different modes of being and are against the status quo. Communities that are just, merciful, inclusive, and hopeful act as signposts for the kind of world we want to inhabit. At their best, they embody the transformative change we want to see happen in the wider society. These communities of resistance and hope needn't only be religious or Christian communities, but can equally be football clubs or other groups for the common good.[13] It's ironic that in Australia the AFL (Australian Football League) is often at the forefront of education and consciousness raising with regard to gay and Indigenous rights. The church and religious communities are either not actively involved or are working against these important changes.

Louis Althusser is a French philosopher who developed the idea of Ideological State Apparatuses (ISAs).[14] These are ostensibly apolitical groups within a society that reinforce the control of the ruling class. Unlike such overt forces as the police or the courts, ISAs are schools, churches, media outlets, and other social insitutitions that buttress the dominant socio-economic narrative and are thus complicit in maintaining the status quo. This is why bringing about change in educational institutions and churches can prove so difficult. We can either to change the institutions we are part of or create new ones.

Small turnings

As noted earlier, Gandhi said change starts with us as individuals; that is, "Be the change you want to see." I rejected a too-narrow version of this idea that doesn't take into account the shift that individuals can undergo as political and cultural change works itself through and transforms local communities. But what happens in individuals can be so profound that it generates significant change in communities and in politics more generally. Gandhi is one example, but we can also think of Martin Luther King Jr. or Greta Thunberg. We needn't end up as famous as they are, but we can start thinking about small changes we might make in our own lives to generate change and transformation.

The idea of "small turnings"—how small things can bring about important changes—comes from a book I read as a young Christian that shaped my thinking. The book was called *Small Turnings,* and it was a call for evangelical Christians to think about making changes in the environment by creating small turnings towards a more just and ecological world. A small turning can take many forms depending on one's context. One way to think about it is by contrasting a small turn with a more significant economic and political change. For example, a major turn would be a carbon emissions trading scheme or carbon tax. A small turning, however, would be a commitment not to use plastic bags, or to install solar panels on your home. A small turning would be to move towards a more plant-based diet. Another example would involve giving money towards World Vision or a similar worthwhile organization, instead of thinking you need to create your own charity or social enterprise.

One of the challenges of living in wealthy areas or countries is that we often find ourselves removed from more obvious forms of suffering. Peter Rollins reminds us that what we really believe is demonstrated by what we do with our time and money. A good way to bring about change in your life is to give to projects that are important to you and that seek to create a more just and ecologically sustainable society. For us as a family, we have chosen certain projects (both locally and internationally) where people are doing significant work in bringing about transformative change in the world. For us this has resulted in giving to the United Nations High Commissioner for Refugees (UNHCR) and the Bill and Melinda Gates Foundation. Locally, we give to cancer research and to palliative care support for children in hospitals in Australia.

Traditionally, Christians have set aside money each month (called a tithe), often around 10% of their income, towards the church. I encourage you to give to the communities you are part of, but also challenge you to think wider and more broadly in terms of setting aside monthly debit orders to organizations working towards goals that are in alignment with your values and faith. Then, at the end of every year, ask yourself, "Can we increase the percentage of our family giving?" The critique of giving money is often that it seeks to assuage guilt and helps us to avoid getting our hands dirty in the day-to-day reality of bringing about change. This is potentially true, and it is certainly a worthwhile question to ask oneself when giving money. I am reminded, though, of the Idiot in Dostoyevsky's book of that title. Someone says to the "Idiot" that they were going to give money to an individual, but then realized they were doing it for the wrong motive—they wanted to be recognized for their good deed. The Idiot suggests that most of the decisions we make in life are filled with double thoughts, but that we should never *not do* a good deed simply because our motives are clouded.[15] In the same way, wanting to do something out of guilt should not stop us engaging in the right act.

The more dangerous proposition is to think that giving money or participating in some communal action should excuse us from the political and structural systems that affect our lives and the lives of others. We could be benefiting from systemic abuse and think our generosity to others excuses us from acting at this level. We should still be generous, but not stop there. We need to think systemically.

Political promise

In this chapter I have been asking you to consider the adventure of a potential encounter with God. I've noted the importance of personal change and decision making, while not neglecting spaces of communal engagement. These are ways to invite a risky adventure with the Divine. They remind us that change is multifaceted and includes the dimensions of religious experience, personal and community life. I also referenced the French philosopher Louis Althusser, and what he termed the "Ideological State Apparatus," or specific cultural and social spaces that influence and change society according to a specific ideological perspective. Althusser saw most of these institutions as negative, but also with the potential to bring about positive change and inculcate positive values. The truth is that there are structural injustices within our society that perpetuate and make life difficult for the Earth and those that inhabit it.

A lot of our cultural and social institutions shape our laws and modes of being. Institutions can define what is appropriate and legal for our behavior. Much of this is important and good, as seen in the protection of private property and prosecuting criminal and violent behavior. Unfortunately, there are also rules and practices that often benefit specific interest groups and sometimes only the wealthy. Christians, and all people for that matter, have different ideas of how we want our communal life and the structures that govern that life to function. Prior to the American Civil War, slavery was constituitional and legal. In the southern states, it was seen as the right way for society and culture to function. In the South Africa that I grew up in, apartheid ensured that whites had certain legal rights and protections, while others did not. In Australia today it is legal to process refugees in offshore detention camps, and in the United States to separate children from their parents at the border. These practices are embodied in institutional laws and regulations.

There are values and beliefs that underpin these structural and legal frameworks. In slavery and apartheid, it was the belief that black people were inferior to white people, and that slavery is ordained in the Bible. There was also the belief that women were not sufficiently intelligent and too emotional to vote, even up to a century ago. In any society there will be different values and beliefs that guide people to think about the best kind of society that they would like, one that would be consistent with their values.

As individuals we might believe that our climate is in peril and that we value the environment. We could choose to install solar panels, eat less meat and, where appropriate, catch public transport. We could further be part of communities or "zones of resistance" that are involved in supporting asylum seekers. We could behave and construct our policies and structures in ways where all people are treated equally—not on the basis of race, culture, religion, or gender. These are important things to do. But to bring about change at a higher level where laws and institutions are reformed—this is politics.

At a political level change can take place (for better or worse) affecting thousands, if not millions, of lives. As a young Christian, I was an avid supporter of the African Christian Democratic Party (ACDP) in South Africa. I was so dedicated that prior to the elections I would go around the neighborhood and take down the posters of other political parties (until I was pulled over by the police!). They never won a large percentage of the vote, but they did end up controlling the balance of power once, and hence got a political appointment of some importance in local government. A group of us were able to meet with this individual and hear him speak about the power of political change. He noted that what could take him his whole life to accomplish as an individual, outside of politics, he was able to make happen with the signature of his pen. This is not always the case, but the point is illuminating.

For many of us, getting involved in politics (or even thinking about it) seems like making a deal with the devil. We see politicians as corrupt and self-serving. Indeed, we might like to think of poly (many) and tic(k)s (blood sucking creatures) as most apt for describing our politicians—blood sucking animals! Of course this is not the case, and there are many good people who serve in politics in order to help their communities and to serve the common good. Often, we only think about political involvement as something that happens during election time and who we might vote for. This is certainly important, particularly for countries that do not have compulsory voting. As my father used to say, "If you don't vote, then don't complain."

The reality, though, is that we cannot neglect the political dimension if we are serious about bringing about change and participating in the adventure with the Divine. New Testament scholar N. T. Wright reminds us that so much of Jesus' teachings concerning the kingdom of God need to be understood against the backdrop of the Roman Empire and the political situation of the time. This is also the case for the apostle Paul, for as Wright says, "When Paul says Jesus is Lord, he means that Caesar is not." [16] Unless we are willing to simply hand over the reins to select interest groups (like the Australian Christian Lobby or the coal mining interests), we need to think more intentionally about how we might bring about structural and legal change in our society. As individuals we might join protest movements against climate change to challenge our politicians to take seriously the issues that are important to us. In Melbourne alone over 100,000 people participated in recent climate protests. So much change takes place when youth are engaged. It was the youth vote that was so instrumental in the plebiscite to legalize same sex marriage in Australia. It is the young people (often under the age of 18) who are driving the climate protests in Australia or seeking to change gun legislation in the United States.

Although it is not unique to the Christian tradition, we have a long history of civil disobedience to draw from. This goes back to the teachings of Jesus in the Beatitudes and the Sermon on the Mount. Even Gandhi credited Jesus for his own inspiration in resisting the British Empire with nonviolence.[17] In Australia, Love Makes a Way is a recent example of how Christians have used civil disobedience and nonviolence to give voice to important issues and to raise concerns regarding structural and legal injustices in the system.[18] Protests and civil disobedience can, and have, brought change to structural injustice. There are also other political avenues for engagement that we might consider.

My choice was to join the Australian Labor party in 2018 at a local branch level. This came about when a Liberal party member (a conservative) was almost elected prime minister after a leadership split within the party. Peter Dutton is someone who is against same sex marriage, has an aggressive refugee and asylum seeker position, and has a terrible record when it comes to indigenous issues in Australia. He was almost our prime minister. Outside of formally running for parliament (which I don't think I'd be particularly good at) I decided to embrace a party that I felt was best placed to bring about change for the good, both structurally and legally, within Australia. Although their policies don't fully align with my values, their values are close to mine. In 2019 they took an enormous risk by bringing to the country an incredibly progressive and just vision for the future of Australia and for our climate. Unfortunately, it was perhaps too much too soon, although I would like to see the party continue with its policy-driven agenda for the common good.[19]

Embodied ethics

Our body is the only home we have in the universe. ~John O'Donohue[20]

Our bodies are fragile, but also incredibly resilient. Our various organs and their interconnections are really a society of actual occasions moving through reality. Sometimes what happens to our bodies, our organs, and cells is out of our control—like when cancer strikes randomly, or when our genetic inheritance works against us. However, research continues to reveal how cancer and other diseases are the result of environmental pollution and degradation, eating habits, and even stress. Prior to my diagnosis, my wife often encouraged (nagged? pestered? forced?) me to eat healthier. Basically, I wanted to eat what I wanted and didn't really care! Following cancer, I began delving deeply into medical research concerning the role of diet in preventing the recurrence rate of my type of cancer. Essentially, my change in diet was a desperate attempt to live longer and enable me to be around for my kids to grow up. Following the perfect diet does not prevent cancer recurrence for everyone, but the statistics are still important in noting the effect of diet on cancer.

Aside from the survival benefits of eating well, John O'Donohue reminds us that our bodies are the only home we have in the universe. In order for me to participate in God's dream for the world, I have chosen to make sure my body is as healthy as possible for as long as I can. The fact that God has been inviting life forward for 13.8 billion years makes me grateful for this short moment. Evolutionarily, so much life has been sacrificed leading to my existence. I should at least be grateful for my body! Ultimately though, looking after your body to avoid suffering and being sick is surely benefit enough.

But there is something deeper here to consider. When we bring about changes in our diet, and in the way we think about that, we bring about changes in ourselves and in the world around us. By actualizing God's values in our dietary choices we can literally embody God's dream for the world. The process ideas of relationality and interconnectedness, along with the affirmation that our present actions influence the future, can now come into sharper focus.

What do I mean by an embodied ethics and changing the world? The acronym that I use for this is called SHE (Sustainability, Health, and Ethics). By choosing to eat sustainably, healthily, and ethically, we change not only ourselves but also the world. This takes seriously the interconnectedness and relational aspect of reality. We are all connected in this adventure called life, while also being responsible for its future direction. In this scenario God's values can be actualized towards a preferred future for the planet. By taking a SHE approach to food we can participate directly in this future. It is literally an ethic that can be embodied.

Sustainability and health

As a species we love eating meat. Before my diagnosis with cancer, I was invited to a friend's birthday at a vegan restaurant. I was horrified and told my wife I might not go! Why would I spend money going out to eat vegetables? Since cancer I have accepted a plant-based diet for myself, and many others are seeing the benefits of such an approach for themselves.

If you are not ready for a plant-based diet, I encourage you to reject meat that is not sustainably farmed, or at least to reduce your meat intake substantially. Globally, livestock contributes 14.5% of anthropogenic greenhouse gases, and 65% of that is directly attributable to beef production.[21] As our population swells to over 10 billion in the next few years, we cannot afford to feed the whole planet on a meat-based diet.[22] Statistics have also shown that the amount of calories you can generate from a plant-based diet, as opposed to a meat-based one, is just not comparable.[23]

If it is important to you that we are able to feed the least fortunate among us, then the question of efficient and sustainable use of our land is crucial. By reducing your meat intake, you have the ability to participate in God's dream for the world at breakfast, lunch, and dinner. This is truly an embodied ethic. You have the ability to change the world and embrace an ethic of sustainability through what you eat.

Aside from addressing climate change through diet, we have the opportunity to reduce our reliance on carbon in our own homes. One of the ways we can do this is by installing solar energy where possible. Again, this seems like a small turning, but small collective acts can begin to make a difference. By installing solar in your home or workplace we can further participate in God's dream for the world.

When the many issues we face seem bewildering, and it is hard to figure out a way forward, it is important to simplify things. By focusing on reducing our meat intake and exploring solar, we have two clear ways to embody our ethics. Both may come at a personal and social cost. Often family and friends find it difficult to understand why you are moving towards a plant-based diet. Solar itself is often not cheap and might require sacrificing other wants in order to be able to afford it.

This raises the issue hinted at throughout this book: which diet is best for a healthy human life? Today there is enormous debate regarding diet, in what could almost be described as "diet wars." Following my operation, and during my chemotherapy, I began to look both generally and specifically at ways I could reduce the potential of my cancer returning. This was prompted by a suggestion from my surgeon that simply by beginning to run I could reduce the risk of cancer returning significantly. My research has borne this out and continues to do so: shifting to a plant-based diet, away from meat and artificial sugars, can produce a significant reduction in cancer recurrence.[24] This is particularly directed towards red meat consumption, to which the World Health Organization has drawn recent attention.[25] Studies continue to emerge showing that cancer amongst young people is on the rise in an unprecedented way. Many believe this is diet related. It makes sense that a diet that prevents cancer from returning would also prevent cancer from occurring in the first place. Of course, one could follow the perfect diet and still get cancer. It is a limiting factor, not a cure-all factor.

Putting red meat through the SHE grid (Sustainability, Health, and Ethics) leads me to the conclusion that it is the right thing to reduce, if not eliminate, its intake. The same would not apply to fish, which most studies indicate is incredibly beneficial for human health. Also, there are some deeper questions that need to be raised about the sustainability of fishing and the ecological devastation taking place in our oceans. The World Count website estimates that if overfishing does not stop, the oceans will run out of fish by 2048.[26]

Ethical explorations (SHE)

Philosopher Daniel Dombrowksi argues that we ought to ask ourselves the following question: If there is no need for us to eat meat, is it ethically fair to kill sentient beings simply for pleasure?[27] For many of us who have been raised in a meat-eating world, such a question raises numerous objections.

Dombrowski asks us to consider the beginning part of the sentence first. He believes that if there is a need to eat meat, as in the case of hunger, or even health, then it is legitimate to do so. For many of us, though, living in first-world contexts, we are able to achieve enough nutrients through a plant-based diet, and this is also more sustainable for the planet and healthier for our bodies.

Some are comfortable eating fish. Others draw the line somewhere around crustaceans. Even if you feel it is ethically legitimate to kill other animals, I urge you to consider how you do so, and the kinds of suffering you feel animals are allowed to go through. Pigs apparently have the intelligence of somewhere between a four-year-old and a fourth grader.[28] Separating baby lambs from their moms for slaughter, and the emotional trauma this causes both mother and the child, is real. Allowing cows and pigs to be factory farmed has been shown to generate high levels of anxiety for the animals involved. I would urge you to at least consider eating animals that have been treated well, both in terms of their environment and the food they eat.

The SHE acronym could be used as a grid to evaluate which foods to eat. Is it sustainable for the planet, healthy for your body, and ethical for the animal? For myself, I have found that the beef industry and red meat consumption does not tick any of the three boxes. Whereas, in my own research, eating free-range organic eggs does. Fish that is sustainably farmed ticks two boxes, but not the ethical question of killing sentient life.

More importantly, the grid can become a tool for participating in God's dream for the world and for embracing an embodied ethic. By rejecting the cattle industry and meat consumption, we can contribute to reducing greenhouse emissions while also freeing up land and water for more efficient production of food and nutrients for the world's poor. By looking after our health, we can, as John O'Donohue reminds us, affirm our body as the only home we have in the universe. By looking after our bodies, we potentially allow ourselves a longer time on this planet to experience and explore all its riches, as well as a longer time to participate with God in the adventure of building a better world. By taking ethics seriously, we affirm all animal life as valued. We can cherish the fact that the mental and emotional suffering of animals is being reduced. As our sciences continue to develop, more and more studies affirm the reality of intelligence and emotional complexity in animals.

Chapter Ten

Embracing the Risk

THE CHRISTIAN tradition is a rich and diverse one. Throughout this book you have been witness to my journey beyond certain aspects of the Christian tradition—one into which I was initiated when I was first captured by the story of Jesus and experienced its imaginative power. It can be easy to dismiss our past, to devalue our inheritance and to deconstruct it. My hope is that, despite my sometimes strong affirmations and statements, you see my journey rather as a reintegration and reformation of my story with different strands of the Christian tradition and process theology. This is consistent with a process metaphysic in general, which believes that all of the past is somehow represented in and influencing the present, but also that the freedom of each moment allows us to respond in fresh, new, and creative ways to that past. By affirming that we, and the universe, are integrated into and related to God panentheistically, my hope is that we feel closer to God than we have ever been. My hope is that we can also value our influence upon God and be receptive to God's influence upon us. This gives impetus to join collaboratively in building better communities and a more just and sustainable planet. Prayer comes alive and becomes powerful as a dynamic and energizing conversation about the future. Prayer changes us, and God. As the traditional doctrines of omnipotence and omniscience are either dropped completely, or readjusted substantially, we can find comfort in a God who is not disconnected and uncaring, but may even be in need of forgiveness. This forgiveness is now extended to us as we seek to partner with God's dream for the world, rather than actively working against it.

My experience of cancer, and the resulting challenges it raised with regards to evolution and the question of theodicy, brought down the house of evangelical cards I had been building. These were the myriad constructions and gymnastics I used to make my version of the Christian experience work. Rather, my illness opened me up to new ways of thinking about the world and generated a theological response. Process theology is a sustained attempt to take evolution and the nature of reality as articulated by science seriously. As Tripp Fuller once said in a podcast, "I'm happy for my faith to go beyond science in its speculation, but not below it."

Process theology seeks to take seriously the fact that the universe is in a process of change and duration, and that it is an event of becoming and interrelatedness. The guides we explored helped us to affirm that both God and the world are panenthestically connected and interrelated. God, the world, and us, move in this process of change and duration together. This allowed us to leave behind traditional conceptions of omniscience and omnipotence, while at the same time enabling us to affirm the potential for religious experience and an encounter with God. This God is one who shares responsibility for the world as it currently stands, hence the difficulty of forgiveness needing to be offered to God. This God, however, is neither all-powerful nor a God who knows every future event. This helps us deal with the problem of evil and the nature of suffering in the world.

God has not left us on our own, though, and, indeed, cannot, as God experiences every event in the world as a collective. God brings God's infinite wisdom and love to bear on each moment of creation and, in a unique way, with human. God invites us to participate in God's dream for the world, for a more just and inclusive reality for all creation. This is where different communities are called upon to participate and pray with God in the midst of this adventure called life, with all its pains and sorrows. In our current time, this leads us to embrace an ecological ethic in order to deal with our planetary emergency. This then results in us embracing not only radical proposals for change, but also small turnings in how we spend our time and money, what we plant, and how we eat (an embodied ethics). We do this not only because of our current crisis, but also because we are interconnected to our planet and its becoming. We do this because God is present everywhere and amongst us all. We do this not only with determination and urgency, but also while resting in the sustaining presence of God's love. The future is open, and it is at risk. But God is not going anywhere and cannot go anywhere. God is fundamentally connected and faithful in God's commitment to the good of the planet and the universe. We can also be faith-full in our response to God and others in each given moment and, by doing so, embrace this risky adventure with the divine.

Endnotes

Chapter One

1. This point is often used to discredit the influence of human-driven climate change. Human beings, however, have destroyed much of the planet through pollution and participated in the extinction of countless animal and plant species. Thus "the atmospheric composition—and, as a result, the climate—seem to be changing faster now than at any time since the last Ice Age and possibly for a lot longer" (Martin Redfern, *The Earth* [Oxford: Oxford University Press, 2003]), 132.

2. Much of our evolutionary nature and heritage was important in getting us to the place where we now are, but they can become evolutionary traps for us going forward. See M. J. Chapman, "Hominid Failings: An Evolutionary Basis for Sin in Individuals and Corporations," in *Evolution and Ethics: Human Morality in Biological and Religious Perspective*, edited by Philip Clayton and Jeffrey Schloss (Grand Rapids, MI: Eerdmans, 2004), 103.

3. Noam Chomsky and George Yancy, "On Trump and the State of the Union," *New York Times*, 5 July 2017, https://www.nytimes.com/2017/07/05/opinion/noam-chomsky-on-trump-and-the-state-of-the-union.html.

4. Alain de Botton touches on these and many other points regarding how the news influences our behavior and vies for our attention. He notes that the "hum and rush of the news has seeped into our deepest selves. What an achievement a moment of calm now is, what a minor miracle the ability to fall asleep or to talk undistracted with a friend—and what monastic discipline would be required to make us turn away from the maelstrom of news and listen for a day to nothing but the rain and our own thoughts" (Alain de Botton, *The News: A User's Manual* [New York: Penguin, 2014]), 16.

5. Yuval Noah Harari, *Homo Deus: A Brief History of Tomorrow* (New York: Harper Collins, 2017), 2.

6. Marcus Borg uses this term to capture the hope inherent in the Christian tradition consistent with the biblical witness. Borg argues that:

> the dream of God is a social and political vision of a world of justice and peace in which human beings do not hurt or destroy, oppress or exploit one another. It is the dream expressed with many images and by many voices in the Bible. . . . The dream of God is a vision of *shalom*, a rich Hebrew word often translated as 'peace' but meaning much more than the absence of war. It means well-being in a comprehensive sense. It includes freedom from negatives such as oppression, anxiety, and fear, as well as the presence of positives such as health, prosperity, and security. *Shalom* thus includes a social vision: the dream of a world in which such well-being belongs to everybody (*The God We Never Knew: Beyond Dogmatic Religion to a More Authentic Faith* [New York: Harper Collins, 2009]), 141.

Chapter Two

1. Hans Küng, *Does God Exist? An Answer for Today* (New York: Doubleday, 1978).

2. James Fowler, *Faith Development and Pastoral Care* (Philadelphia: Fortress Press, 1987) 101.

3. Apartheid argued that black and white people should have separate spheres of development, with different territorial divisions. The South African president D. F. Malan argued that the policy was one in which "each population group could develop its ambitions and capabilities to the fullest" (*South Africa in the 20th Century*, ed. S. B. Spies and B. J. Liebenberg [Pretoria: Van Schaik, 1993]), 322.

4. See Pam Christie and Carolyn McKinney, "Decoloniality and 'Model C' Schools: Ethos, Language and the Protests of 2016":

    "The establishment of Model C schools dates back to the dying days of apartheid, when the politically dominant National Party took steps to protect white schools—the best resourced in the system—in the face of impending change that would necessarily see the end of racially based privilege. In 1990, in the context of political transition, the apartheid government developed a set of governance options for white schools that would pass substantial powers to the parent bodies of these schools and allow them to admit students of other races under strict conditions" (*Education as Change* 21.3 [2017], 1–21, https://dx.doi.org/10.17159/1947-9417/2017/2332).

5. Jason Burke and Vincent Lalit "We Are a Special Country: South Africa Hopes World Cup Win Can Bring Unity," *The Guardian*, 3 November 2019, https://www.theguardian.com/sport/2019/nov/03/south-africa-hopes-rugby-world-cup-win-can-bring-unity-ramaphosa-desmond-tutu.

6. I relate to the South African theologian John De Gruchy's account of conversion within the South African context, "I made a commitment to Jesus Christ as saviour and Lord at a Christian youth camp ... However others might assess it now, whether psychologically or theologically, it was a decision that affected the rest of my life" (*Being Human: Confessions of a Christian Humanist* [London: SCM Press, 2006]).

Chapter Three

1. Classically stated, theodicy asks the question: if God is all-good and all-powerful, why is there evil?

2. This is something that philosopher Alain de Botton has written about extensively. He makes the argument that, philosophically and sociologically, happiness is unrelated to the pursuit of money and power, but that one of its key components comes down to relationships. See Alain de Botton, *The Consolations of Philosophy* (London: Penguin, 2000). De Botton offers a more detailed analysis in a later book, where he argues that status anxiety cripples us from making the changes in our lives that we need to make (*Status Anxiety* [London: Penguin, 2004]).

3. A populist account, but certainly a worthy one, is by Mark Manson, in which he reminds us is that a majority of the time most people are concerned with themselves and not us! Hence, we should be less anxious about what others think of us. See Mark Manson, *The Subtle Art of Not Giving a F*ck* (San Francisco: Harper One, 2016).

4. Many traditions have sought to use the awareness of one's death as a motivation for rethinking our responsibilities. A Buddhist proverb I have found helpful is the following: "Your time is uncertain; your death is certain. What will you do?"

5. It's important to note again that cancer recurrence is a complex issue, and there are many things that can contribute to it. One

can never completely guard against a recurrence but can lessen the odds.

6. John O' Donohue, *Anam Cara: Spiritual Wisdom from the Celtic World* (New York: Bantam Books, 1997), 69.

Chapter Four

1. Early research in cognitive dissonance was conducted by Leon Festinger. See Leon Festinger, *A Theory of Cognitive Dissonance* (Redwood City, CA: Stanford University Press, 1957). Confirmation bias was demonstrated decisively by Peter Wason. See Peter Wason, "Reasoning, " in *New Horizons in Psychology*, ed. B. Foss, Vol.20 (1966): 135–51; and "Reasoning about a Rule," *Quarterly Journal of Experimental Psychology* 20 (1968): 273–81.

2. Much of this section is taken from an article published in *Process Studies* and used with permission. See Brian Macallan, "Cancer and Theodicy: a Personal Reflection," *Process Studies* 46.2 (2017).

3. John Polkinghorne, *The Polkinghorne Reader: Science, Faith and the Search for Meaning*, ed. T. J. Oord (London: SPCK, 2010), 141.

4. Carl Jung, *Memories, Dreams, Reflections* (New York: Vintage, 1989), 69.

5. Cary Funk and Lee Rainie, Public and Scientists' Views on Science and Society, Pew Research Center, 29 Jan. 2015, https://www.pewresearch.org/science/2015/01/29/public-and-scientists-views-on-science-and-society/.

6. Special Nielsen Poll: Faith in Australia 2009, 16 Dec. 2009.

7. Hans Küng, *Credo: The Apostles' Creed Explained for Today* (London: SCM Press, 1993).

8. Brian Macallan, "The Küng Is Dead, Long Live the Küng: The Value of Hans Küng's Theology," *HTS Theological Studies* 78.4 a7632 (2022), https://doi.org/10.4102/hts.v78i4.7632.

9. John Stott, *Understanding the Bible* (Berkshire, UK: Scripture Union, 1972).

10. C. S. Lewis, *Mere Christianity* (London: Fount, 1942), 171–73.

11. Alistair McGrath, *A Fine-Tuned Universe: The Quest for God in Science and Theology* (Louisville, KY: Westminster John Knox Press, 2009), 199.

12. Two recent volumes have engaged in both Christian and non-Christian reflections on the role of evolution in the origin of life and the implications for morality. See *Biology, Ethics, and the Origins of Life*, ed. Rolston Holmes III (Belmont, CA: 1995), as well as *Evolution and Ethics,* Philip Clayton and Jeffrey Schloss, Grand Rapids, MI: Eerdman's, 2004).

13. The zoologist Andrew Parker, one of the foremost scholars of the Big Bang, has argued that light was crucial to this evolutionary moment. Interestingly, Parker has written a book exploring the parallels with the Genesis account and the process of evolution, although I remain unconvinced. See Andrew Parker, *The Genesis Enigma* (London: Penguin, 2010).

14. For more on this topic, see John Hick, *Evil and the God of Love* (New York: Harper and Row, 1975), 369–70.

15. David Hume, *Dialogues Concerning Natural Religion* (London: Penquin Books, 1990), 108–09.

16. Fyodor Dostoevsky, *The Brothers Karamazov* (London: Penguin, 1993), 320–21.

17. Albert Camus, *The Rebel* (Middlesex, UK: Penguin, 1974), 50.

18. For more on this topic, see, Gustaf Aulén, *A Historical Study of the Three Main Types of Atonement* (London: SPCK, 1956). C. S. Lewis considered this one of his favorite books.

19. N. T. Wright, *Surprised by Scripture: Engaging Contemporary Issues* (New York: Harper Collins, 2015), 37–39.

20. Peter Enns, *The Evolution of Adam: What the Bible Does and Doesn't Say about Human Origins* (Grand Rapids, MI: Brazos, 2012).

21. Enns, *Evolution of Adam*, 120–21.

22. Hans Jonas, "The Concept of God after Auschwitz: A Jewish Voice," in *Readings in Philosophy of Religion: East Meets West*, ed. A. Eshleman (Hoboken, NJ: Blackwell, 2008), 270.

23. Dale Migliore, *Faith Seeking Understanding: An Introduction to Christian Theology* (Grand Rapids, MI: Eerdmans, 2004), 155.

24. Krista Tippett, "The Tragedy of the Believer," On Being, 13 July 2006, https://onbeing.org/programs/elie-wiesel-tragedy-believer-2/.

25. John Crossan, *The Historical Jesus: The Life of a Mediterranean Jewish Peasant* (New York: Harper, 1991).

26. N. T. Wright, *Jesus and the Victory of God* (London: SPCK, 1996).

27. Dale Allison, *Jesus of Nazareth: Millenarian Prophet* (Minneapolis: Fortress, 1998).

28. Rudolph Bultmann, *Faith and Understanding*, Vol. 1 (London: SCM, 1969), 132.

29. Pierre Teilhard de Chardin, *The Phenomenon of Man* (New York: Harper and Row, 1965).

Chapter Five

1. Didier Debaise, *Nature as Event* (Durham: Duke University Press, 2017).

2. See Jay McDaniel, "The Greening of China," *Worldviews* 12, (2008).

3. This can be seen in Helmut Maaßen's book series on European Studies in Process Thought and in the formation of various

associations in the last few years, both in the United Kingdom, the Association for Process Thought, and on the continent, the European Society for Process Thought.

4. Keith Ansell-Pearson has shown that this renaissance in Bergson's thinking is being applied to new research in philosophy of mind, philosophy of time, and philosophy of biology. See Keith Ansell-Pearson, *Bergson: Thinking Beyond the Human Condition* (London: Bloomsbury, 2018), 1.

5. There are numerous texts one could cite to illustrate this point. What follows is a small sample: Didier Debaise, *Speculative Empiricsm: Revisiting Whitehead* (Edinburgh: Edinburgh University Press, 2017); Isabelle Stengers, *Thinking with Whitehead: A Free and Wild Creation of Concepts* (Cambridge, MA: Harvard University Press, 2014); Fabrice Bothereau; *Des compositions de l'experience Whitehead, l'hylemorphisme et le phenomene* (Bucharest: Zeta Books, 2015); and *Deleuze, Whitehead, Bergson: Rhizomatic Connections,* ed. Keith Robinson (New York: Palgrave Macmillan, 2009).

6. Clark Pinnock, Richard Rice, John Sanders, William Hasker and David Basinger, *The Openness of God: A Biblical Challenge to the Traditional Understanding of God* (Downers Grove, IL: IVP Academic, 1994).

7. John B. Cobb, Jr. and David Ray Griffin, *Process Theology: An Introductory Exposition* (Philadephia: Westminster, 1976), 156, 159.

8. Large portions of this section appeared in a previous journal article and are used here with permission. See Brian Macallan: "Getting off the Omnibus: Rejecting Free Will and Soul-Making Responses to the Problem of Evil," *Open Theology* 6, 1 (2020).

9. Dale Allison, *The Luminous Dusk: Finding God in the Deep Still Places* (Grand Rapids, MI: Eerdmans, 2006), 150.

10. Charles Hartshorne may be best known for naming this. See his

Omnipotence and Other Theological Mistakes (Albany: SUNY, 1984), 25.

11. David Ray Griffin, *Panentheism and Scientific Naturalism* (Claremont, CA: Process Century Press, 2014), 122. One of the key insights of process theism is its rejection of the idea that coercive power is the highest form of power. An all-powerful God who does, or could, constantly intervene in the world would raise some real challenges as to the goodness of God (Philip Clayton and S. Knapp, *The Predicament of Belief: Science, Philosophy, and Faith* [Oxford: Oxford University Press, 2011], 123–27). Process theism argues that God lures us towards the future with a power that is persuasive (Zachary Simpson and Philip Clayton, *Adventures in the Spirit* [Minneapolis: Fortress Press, 2008], 224–25).

12. The full quotation is: "The only liveable doctrine of divine power is that it influences all that happens and determines nothing in its concrete particularity," Hartshorne, *Omnipotence*, 25.

13. Stephen Evans and Zachary Manis, *Philosophy of Religion: Thinking about Faith* (Downers Grove, IL: InterVarsity Press, 2009), 133.

14. David Ray Griffin, *Evil Revisited: Responses and Considerations* (New York: SUNY Press, 1991), 24.

15. See Hartshorne, *Omnipotence*, 9; and Daniel Dombrowski, *Whitehead's Religious Thought: From Mechanism to Organism, from Force to Persuasion* (New York: SUNY Press, 2017), 137.

16. John Hick, *Evil and the God of Love* (Norfolk, VA: Collins, 1975).

17. Griffin, *Evil*, 81–83.

18. Griffin, *Evil*, 30.

19. "Cosmological constants" refers to the fundamental laws of physics required to reproduce, in its entirety, a universe indistinguishable from this one.

20. Stephen Jay Gould, *Wonderful Life: The Burgess Shale and the History of Nature* (New York: Norton and Co., 1990).

21. This is the argument that the scientist Simon Conway-Morris makes in his book *Life's Solution: Inevitable Humans in a Lonely Universe* (Cambridge, UK: Cambridge University Press, 2003).

Chapter Six

1. For a discussion of the tragedy of the Church's condemnation of Galileo, see Hans Küng, *Does God Exist?* (New York: Doubleday, 1978), 9–10.

2. Alister McGrath, *A Fine-Tuned Universe: The Quest for God in Science and Theology* (Louisville: Westminster John Knox, 2009), 199.

3. The term "radical empiricism" comes from William James. The *relations between* things are as real as the particulars of a thing that can be seen, felt, tasted, etc., and cannot be omitted from a description of the thing.

4. An excellent example of this is Philip Clayton's description of the initial conditions of the universe and the inferences we can make about God on the basis of this. See Philip Clayton and Steven Knapp, *The Predicament of Belief: Science, Philosophy, Faith* (Oxford: Oxford University Press, 2011).

5. Although I disagree with Richard Dawkins' assessment of the metaphysical implications of the evidence, I do agree with his assessment of the reality of evolution. The comment the "greatest show on earth" is a reference to Dawkins' *The Greatest Show on Earth: the Evidence for Evolution* (London: Random House, 2009).

6. John Jungermann, "Evidence for Process in the Physical World," in Timothy E. Eastman and Hank Keeton, *Physics and Whitehead: Quantum, Process and Experience* (New York: SUNY, 2003), 72.

7. Notwithstanding the Flat Earth Society!
8. Krista Tippett, Interview with Carlo Rovelli, *All Reality is Interaction,* On Being, 16 March 2017, https://onbeing.org/programs/carlo-rovelli-all-reality-is-interaction/.
9. Carlo Rovelli, *The Order of Time* (London: Penguin, 2017), 86–87.
10. John Jungermann "Evidence for Process," 53.
11. Debaise, *Nature as Event* (London: Duke University Press, 2017), 29.
12. Debaise, *Nature,* 42.
13. Jungermann, *Evidence,* 47. "According to the general theory of relativity, there is an interdependence of time, space, mass-energy, and gravity. They are all interlinked. Time is itself part of a process." The general theory also predicts that accelerating masses will give off gravitational radiation—a prediction recently verified with great precision by long-term observation of a binary pulsar.
14. Carlo Rovelli, *Helgoland: Making Sense of the Quantum Revolution,* ed. Erica Segre and Simon Carnell (New York: Riverhead Books, 2021).-
15. For a detailed discussion of the goldilocks effect see Paul Davies, *The Goldilocks Enigma: Why the Universe Is Just Right for Life* (London: Penguin, 2006).
16. Jungermann, *Evidence,* 51.
17. Lee Smolin, *Time Reborn: from the Crisis in Physics to the Future of the Universe* (London: Penguin, 2013), xvii.

Chapter Seven

1. Catherine Keller, *On the Mystery: Discerning Divinity in Process* (Philadelphia: Fortress, 2008), 61.

2. Charles Hartshorne, *Omnipotence and Other Theological Mistakes* (Albany: SUNY, 1984), 38–39.

3. Robert Gnuse, *The Old Testament and Process Theology* (St. Louis: Chalice Press, 2000), 4.

4. Gen. 1:2.

5. Catherine Keller, *Political Theology of the Earth: Our Planetary Emergency and the Struggle for a New Public* (New York: Columbia University Press, 2018), 138.

6. Keller, *Political Theology*, 146.

7. Catherine Keller, *God and Power: Counter Apocalyptic Journeys* (Minneapolis: Fortress, 2004), 31.

8. Oliver Sacks, *The River of Consciousness* (London: Picador, 2017), 70.

9. Krista Tippett, Interview with Carlo Rovelli, *All Reality is Interaction,* On Being, 16 March 2017, https://onbeing.org/programs/carlo-rovelli-all-reality-is-interaction/.

10. Paul Davies, *The Goldilocks Enigma: Why Is the Universe Just Right for Life?* (London: Penguin, 2006).

11. For an exploration of the rationality of the world and the tentative endorsement of this view see, Paul Davies, *The Mind of God: the Scientific Basis for a Rational World* (New York: Simon and Schuster, 1993).

12. Colin McGinn, *The Mysterious Flame: Conscious Minds in a Material World* (New York: Basic Books, 1999).

13. Daniel Dennett, *Consciousness Explained* (New York: Back Bay Books, 1991).

14. Thomas Nagel, *Mind and Cosmos* (Oxford: Oxford University Press, 2012), 95.

15. David Chalmers, *The Character of Consciousness* (Oxford:

Oxford University Press, 2010), 103.

16. Dombrowski, Daniel, *Whitehead's Religious Thought: from Mechanism to Organism, from Force to Persuasion* (New York: SUNY Press, 2017), 11.

17. Dombrowski, *Whitehead's Religious Thought*, 16.

18. Krista Tippett, Interview with John O'Donohue, *The Inner Landscape of Beauty*, 28 February, 2008, https://onbeing.org/programs/john-odonohue-the-inner-landscape-of-beauty-aug2017/.

19. ScienceDaily, "They Remember: Communities of Microbes Found to Have Working Memory," 28 April 2020, www.sciencedaily.com/releases/2020/04/200428093506.htm (from materials provided by University of California San Diego, original written by Mario Aguilera).

20. Peter Wohlleben, *The Hidden Life of Trees: What they Feel, How they Communicate* (Vancouver: Greystone Books, 2015); Peter Godfrey-Smith, *Other Minds: The Octopus, the Sea and the Deep Origins of Consciousness* (New York: Farrar, Straus and Giroux, 2016).

21. Didier Debaise, *Nature as Event: The Lure of the Possible* (London: Duke University Press, 2017), 2.

22. David Ray Griffin, *Panentheism and Scientific Naturalism* (Claremont, CA: Process Century Press, 2014), 14.

23. Griffin, *Panentheism*, 23.

24. Acts 17:28.

25. Frederik Beiser, *Hegel* (New York: Routledge, 2005), 143–45

26. To see how a panentheistic approach can be connected with the reality of suffering and pain see, Jürgen Moltmann, *God in Creation* (Minneapolis: Fortress, 1993).

27. See David Ray Griffin, *Re-enchantment without Supernaturalism:*

A Process Theology of Religion (New York: Cornell University Press, 2000).

28. Griffin, *Panentheism*, 34–35.
29. Philip Clayton, editor, *The Oxford Handbook of Religion and Science* (Oxford: Oxford University Press, 2006).
30. Zachary Simpson and Philip Clayton, *Adventures in the Spirit: God, World, Divine Action* (Minneapolis: Fortress, 2008), 93.
31. Philip Clayton, *Mind and Emergence: from Quantum to Consciousness* (Oxford: Oxford University Press, 2004).
32. Philip Clayton and Steven Knapp, *The Predicament of Belief: Science, Philosophy, and Faith* (Oxford: Oxford University Press, 2011.
33. Simpson and Clayton, *Adventures in the Spirit*, 187–88.
34. Clayton, *Mind and Emergence*, 203.

Chapter Eight

1. Bruce Epperly, *Process Theology: a Guide for the Perplexed* (New York: Continuum, 2011).
2. Peter Singer, *Hegel: a Very Short Introduction* (Oxford: Oxford University Press, 1983), 106.
3. Alfred North Whitehead, *Process and Reality*, corrected edition, ed. David Ray Griffin and Donald W. Sherburne ([1929] New York: The Free Press, 1978), 351.
4. Whitehead suggests two ways to think about God: as having a primordial and a consequent nature. God's primordial nature is the everlasting source of value and possibility. God's consequent nature "interacts with the world . . . [feeling] fully every single actual occasion in the world. . . . This consequent nature of God is the aspect of God that is continuously changing as the world changes." See https://iep.utm.edu/processp/.

5. Philip Clayton and Steven Knapp, *The Predicament of Belief: Science, Philosophy, and Faith* (Oxford: Oxford University Press, 2011) 153.

6. Hans Jonas, "The Concept of God after Auschwitz: A Jewish Voice," in *Mortality and Morality: A Search for the Good after Auschwitz,"* ed. and trans. Lawrence Vogel (Evanston, IL: Northwestern University, 1996), 134.

7. Jürgen Moltmann, quoting Elie Wiesel, *Night* (1955). The full quote is as follows:

> The SS hanged two Jewish men and a youth in front of the whole camp. The men died quickly, but the death throes of the youth lasted for half an hour. "Where is God? Where is he?" someone asked behind me. As the youth still hung in torment in the noose after a long time I heard the man call again, "Where is God now?" And I heard a voice in myself answer: "Where is *he*? He is here. He is hanging there on the gallows."

Moltmann continues:

> "Any other answer would be blasphemy. There cannot be any other Christian answer to the question of this torment. To speak here of a God who could not suffer would make God a demon. To speak here of an absolute God would make God an annihilating nothingness. To speak here of an indifferent God would condemn men to indifference" (*The Crucified God* (London: SCM], 273–74).

Chapter Nine

1. Marcus Borg, *The God We Never Knew: Beyond Dogmatic Religion to a More Authentic Faith* (New York: Harper Collins, 2009), 141.

2. Rev.21:1-4: Then I saw "a new heaven and a new earth," for the first heaven and the first earth had passed away, and there was no longer any sea. I saw the Holy City, the new Jerusalem, coming down out of heaven from God, prepared as a bride beautifully dressed for her husband. And I heard a loud voice from the throne saying, "Look! God's dwelling place is now among the people, and he will dwell with them. They will be his people, and God himself will be with them and be their God. 'He will wipe every tear from their eyes. There will be no more death' or mourning or crying or pain, for the old order of things has passed away."

3. N. T. Wright, *The New Testament and the People of God* (Minneapolis: Fortress, 1996), 333.

4. See Pinnock, et al, *The Openness of God: A Biblical Challenge to the Traditional Understanding of God* (Downers Grove, IL InterVarsity Press, 1994).

5. Yuval Harari, *Sapiens: A Brief History of Humankind* (London: Harvill Seeker, 2015), 71–75.

6. Jacob Poushter, Moira Fagan, and Christine Huang, "Americans Are Less Concerned—But More Divided—on Climate Change than People Elsewhere," Pew Research Center, 14 September 2021, https://www.pewresearch.org/short-reads/2021/09/14/americans-are-less-concerned-but-more-divided-on-climate-change-than-people-elsewhere/.

7. Martin Redfern, *The Earth: A Very Short History* (Oxford: Oxford University Press, 2003).

8. Summary for Policymakers, IPCC Special Report: Global Warming of 1.5°C, https://www.ipcc.ch/sr15/chapter/spm/.

9. Gerado Marti, "The Unexpected Orthodoxy of Donald J. Trump: White Evangelical Support for the 45th President of the United States," *Sociology of Religion* 80, no.1 (2019): 1–8.

10. Willem Saayman, *Church Mission in South Africa: Political and Ecumenical* (Pretoria: University of South Africa, 1991).

11. Rodney Stark, *The Rise of Christianity* (New York: Harper Collins, 1997.) 84.

12. 1 Cor. 11:17-34.

13. Andrew Menzies and Dean Phelan, *Kingdom Communities: Shining the Light of Christ through Faith, Hope and Love* (Eugene, OR: Wipf and Stock, 2018).

14. Louis Althusser, "Idéologie et appareils idéologiques d'État (Notes pour une recherche)," *La Pensée* No.151 (1970): 67–125.

15. Fyodor Dostoevsky, *The Idiot* (Hertfordshire, UK: Wordsworth, 1996), 290.

16. N. T. Wright, "Paul and Caesar: A New Reading of Romans. Originally published in *A Royal Priesthood? The Use of the Bible Ethically and Politically*, ed. C. Bartholemew, J. Chaplin, R. Song, and A. Wolters (Grand Rapids, MI: Zondervan, 2002), 173–93.

17. For a detailed assessment of Gandhi's nonviolence in relation to Christianity, see Terrance Rynne, *Gandhi and Jesus: the Saving Power of Non-violence* (Maryknoll, NY: Orbis, 2008).

18. https://actionnetwork.org/groups/love-makes-a-way-australia.

19. For the argument that the Labor party should stick to this progressive agenda, see: Adrian Pabst, *Story of our Country* (Brisbane: Connor Court Publishing, 2019).

20. John O' Donahue, *Anam Cara* (New York: Bantam Books, 1997), 69.

21. https://www.fao.org/news/story/en/item/197623/icode/.

22. Bingli Clark Chai, Johannes Reidar van der Voort, Kristina Grofelnik, Helga Gudny Eliasdottir, Ines Klöss, and Federico

J. A. Perez-Cueto, "Which Diet Has the Least Environmental Impact on Our Planet? A Systematic Review of Vegan, Vegetarian and Omnivorous Diets," *Sustainability* No. 11 (2019).

23. David Pimentel and Marcia Pimentel, "Sustainability of Meat-based and Plant-based Diets and the Environment," *The American Journal of Clinical Nutrition* 78, no. 3 (2003): 660–63.

24. Amy Lanou and Barbara Svenson, "Reduced Cancer Risk in Vegetarians: An Analysis of Recent Reports," *Cancer Management Research* 3 (2011): 1–18.

25. Veronique Bouvard, Dana Loomis, Kathyrn Guyton, Yann Grosse, Fatiha El Ghissassi, Lamia Benbrahim-Tallaa, Neela Guha, Heidi Mattock, Kurt Straif, "Carcinogenicity of Consumption of Red and Processed Meat," *Lancet Oncology* 16, no.16 (2015): 1599–600.

26. https://www.theworldcounts.com/challenges/planet-earth/oceans/overfishing-statistics.

27. Daniel Dombrowski, *Philosophy of Vegetarianism* (Amherst: Masschusetts University Press, 1984).

28. See Evan Malmgren, "The Intelligence of Swine, https://www.noemamag.com/the-intelligence-of-swine/.

www.ingramcontent.com/pod-product-compliance
Lightning Source LLC
Chambersburg PA
CBHW030527080526
44586CB00011B/347